Angelina - sp. challeng
        praise = ep ic

Janice - praise a new g/child.
    Hugh - 9yrs - talk to him about birth dad.

michelle - praise dog daycare
        Sp got job @ butcher in Vons

Vicky - son City Heights Brian + Shell
        better relat. w/him.

Tyler + Shawntee - bby in Nov. (Mila) girl

Brandi - hyperthyroid - figure it out

Do u have peace? If not, go to Word
and get peace back.   Matt 11: 28-30
            matt 10:1   yoke, burden
Pray w/ authority   Luke 10:19
Make choice to believe, stand on it! Lay the burdens
Mind Mind - discipline, go to Word.
renew + Heal my mind - Pray this. Take authority over it.
Phil 4: 9, 11, 13
Be aware of what is going in w/mind
    My purpose in Christ today?

10/11/21 Pastor Jim →
Survive to thrive ⟷ Bold

Janice & Duncan - mom's sustain/balance
90th B-day - her mm.
Spoke to Andy - went awesome about Hugh.
anxiety about future, feel can't do it.

Praises for Brandi & Steve - truck, church
sowing seeds.

Julie + David =   Glen
    bad accident for bro in motorcycle accid
Supernatural peace for him - rehab
need provisin. insur. wife & 2 boys.

Staci - + = complete time together. prayer = dtr - going   Zoe - 26
                                                 thru stuff.
                                        pray 4 me = get out
Reigh - + = men's bible study   of way so God can
         is awesome!   do this thing.
Theresa - watching over parents, the stress, ↑
bld pressure. navigate 2 households.
Ray & Kathleen = parents. Refining.
Praise - son going to FaisHouse - in men's ministry
Fear = to die = Her dad. Want to ✓ont.

Angelina - sp getting better, slow but sure. wants
his bed. He had God moment. Victor = sp.
ø back issue rite now.

Michelle - praises w/sponse - job & men's ministry
         do dog job full time? Hair - give up?

Stand on the Word, take authority.
Let it go - parents, kids.
Matt 10:1 & 10:8 we have authority-take it.
Pray healing over ur mind. Go to Bible
Clear & Light in mind & thoughts
What If's come-Rebuke immedtly.

In the Great

I AM

1/24/22   God u r my thought process
Complete dep on God or Indep from

God?

Anthony A. Casillas

J. gave us His authority. Share everything w/ God.
Deep relat. w/ JC. Make a choice
1 Peter 4:2
Whatever you feed, grows. Stay out of ur own way
ut feet in grass & be still for 15 min.

God said to Moses, "I AM WHO I AM." And he said,
"Say this to the people of Israel, I AM has sent me to you."

- Exodus 3:14 (ESV)

"These words and commentary have been written through the inspiration of the Holy Spirit and the Grace of my Lord and Savior Jesus Christ."

Anthony A. Casillas
Ambassador for Jesus Christ

Table of Contents

My Purpose

My spirit was inspired and led by my Lord and Savior Jesus Christ, through the Holy Spirit, to write this book. I wanted to share what is in my heart and in my spirit, through the Holy Spirit, with those who may be searching for some insight on their purpose and truth in their lives, and to tell them how I believe Jesus Christ is the true answer for all those who believe. I trust the Lord with all my heart, I love my Father in heaven, my Lord Jesus Christ, and the Holy Spirit with all that I have been given through grace from God through Jesus Christ. I am stepping out in faith to walk down this path and take this journey with all of you, in and through faith in Jesus Christ.

For as long as I can remember, I have been asking myself the question about what is my true purpose and walk in Christ. How exactly do I dwell in His truth for my life and manifest Christ's glory in everything I do, and express it with all the people that I touch on a daily basis? With this question in mind, I prayed to God through Jesus Christ and asked Him to show me His way to my own walk and my own purpose in Christ. For a long time, I was being tossed all over the place and I didn't understand that my struggles had meaning and purpose in God's plan for me as a true adopted child of God through faith in Christ Jesus.

I realized very quickly in my walk in Jesus Christ that I was flowing towards Christ even before I was "born again" in Christ. I have always been drawn to my Lord Jesus Christ, even when I was a young boy, although I hadn't reached the point where I became a new creation in Christ, through grace, till later in my life. Even as a young Christian, I still fell into sin and fell short in my walk in Christ. But I soon began to realize, as I was guided to write this book, that everything in all of our lives has purpose in Christ. We might not fully understand it most of the time, but through His measure of faith that is given to all believers, we realize that it is all part of the grand plan of our Father in heaven. Don't get me wrong, I have always been totally amazed at how God has worked in my life, even to this very moment, while writing these inspired words to and for you. I am just a normal man that has never written a book before, but I am now a man of God, "so all things are possible for those who believe" Mark 9:23. I still ask myself this question- for what reason and how exactly is this all going to work for those who are chosen by God to read my words and commentary, and hear my testimony? I always come to be assured by the Holy Spirit that the Lord Jesus Christ and God are in control and His grace will show me the path and also show the path to those who are to receive these words.

The foundation of this book is the scripture from *The Holy Bible, English Standard Version (ESV)*. This is purposeful and, I believe, is directed and anointed through the Holy Spirit. For every topic and for all the chapters, the foundation is the scripture from the gospel and the incredibly powerful good news it brings. Scripture is not about what man says, but is "breathed out by God" 2 Timothy 3:16, through the

Holy Spirit to those who were appointed by God to share His truth through the prophets and the apostles of Jesus Christ and God. The beauty of this opportunity, for me, was the manifestation of the 'Word' as the only truth in my life that I could truly count on, for my purpose and walk in Christ through grace.

What I have done in this book is to give a true account of different times in my life, and to share with all of you my testimony of how God, in every instance, was in direct control of my life. I will parallel those moments in my life with the 'Word' of God. I have come to understand that God has always been, and will always be, in command of my life through faith in Jesus Christ, even when I had lost my way. God is always running after all of us, even when we make choices that are against His plan and in opposition to our true purpose for our lives. God always has a way for His children.

The true gift for me, in writing this book, was to be able to look back into my past and gather an understanding of my truth in Christ, and share some of those things with all of you to let you know just how much Jesus Christ has changed and saved my life. I believe my life is another example of one of God's miracles in Jesus Christ, so if you are looking for a miracle here I am. I have been in a lot of prayer while writing this book, which has been a gift in itself. Through the guidance of the Holy Spirit, I was able to discern what I was to write about. I also prayed about the scriptures that would be given to me by the Holy Spirit to touch your lives. These Scriptures have also guided me through my testimony and have given me enlightenment through this commentary. I am not a professional author, but the words in this book have flowed from my fingertips through the revelation of the scripture in my heart, through the Holy Spirit. The gift of Scripture is something that, I pray, will touch your lives in a strong way, if it hasn't already.

I believe part of my purpose and truth in Christ is being manifested through the writing of these words, and also through what grace has done for me in my spirit and in my life by walking in faith in Jesus Christ. I love to encourage others and I believe it is one of the gifts that have been apportioned to me from God and Jesus Christ through the Holy Spirit. 1 Peter 4:10 states, "As each has received a gift, use it to serve one another, as good stewards of God's varied grace." I realize that I have been given this inspiration and purpose so that this message can touch others in a powerful way when I share about Jesus Christ and His grace and the good news of salvation with others. I am praying that those who are led to read these words are encouraged and touched spiritually by this opportunity to get to know Jesus Christ and the gift of salvation. And for those that already have a relationship with Jesus Christ, I am praying that they would carry on in their walk and faith that God is always working in their lives through Jesus Christ, and that they continue to walk in their truth and purpose in Jesus Christ. It is such a blessing to touch others through the gifts that God has given to me through Christ. So I thank you, and I pray that your truth and purpose will be realized through the Holy Spirit and your faith in Jesus Christ, and all the gifts that God has given to you will shine onto others.

Dwell in His grace and trust that God is in control of your life, and love others, and walk in the truth *'In the Great I Am.'*

Blessings to all of you,
Anthony A. Casillas

CHAPTER 1

My Childhood Testimony (God's Miracles in My Life)

From as early on as I can remember, I realized that I was going to have to learn to survive and persevere in my life. I felt as if I was continually being hurt and neglected by the people that I trusted and loved the most in my life. I know this a heavy way to start this book, but I wanted you all to know the truth about where I was when I was younger, compared to where I am today. This book is a testimony of my truth in Jesus Christ.

When I was a four year old little boy I remember being in constant fear of making my father unhappy or angry for some reason or another. I would do everything in my power, from morning to night, to avoid my father's discipline. This included staying in my room even when I had to go to the bathroom as that could've disturbed him and not been good for me. I learned about fear at a very early age in life, and it tormented me for a long time. My family was always on the move, from one place to another, and I was never able to make and keep friends for very long. As a young boy I was so hurt and scared all the time. My feelings were so beyond my understanding that I was basically living in survival mode, and by instinct, for as long as I can remember. The truth about my challenges and the subsequent consequences would not truly be manifested or fully understood until later on in my life.

There is one particular memory, that I'd like to share with all of you, that really represents what my young life looked like for me. I was in a new school and I remember being so lost and isolated from everyone that I just wanted to run away. One day I found myself walking out of this new school I was attending, at barely 6 years of age and in first grade, and getting on a city bus in Los Angeles, California. I sat down and got driven around the city in this bus for most of the morning, until I finally got off where I had gotten on the bus originally. The truly sad part of this story is that not one person had even noticed on the bus that I was all by myself. Can you imagine a little 6 year old boy riding a city bus all by himself for hours, and not even one person, including the bus driver, noticing this little boy? I certainly can't, and to this day it hurts my heart and makes me emotional because of the truth of this story and because of how many other little kids might be feeling like this. An even greater tragedy in this story is that not even one person, including my teacher, had realized that I was not still in class or school that morning. Not one person on the city bus or in my elementary school had even asked me if I needed help, not one! It was as if I was invisible. In my eyes I was truly invisible to everyone around me.

Not until many years later, when I spoke of the incident to my mother had anyone known about this incident, because I had kept it a secret. This was the truly sad world that I was living in when I was a young boy. I now believe that God knew where I was, and protected me every second during that morning's adventure on the bus. I could've been kidnapped, or hurt, or gotten lost and maybe never came back. This is the *first miracle of God saving me* that I can remember, but it is one of those memories that has stuck with me till this day.

This is an important aspect of what my life was and what it has become. The truth is that God was always a part of my life, from the very first moment that He decided to create me. When we are 6 years old, we may or may not have an understanding of this truth. But as I look back on this story, it is very apparent to me that God was, and is still, working in every moment of my life. God is sovereign in my life even when I make bad choices. God is always good and provides me with a path back to His purpose even when I get off course, and I am so thankful for His love in my life.

There were times in my young life when I was unsure if my parents would stay together, and in fact I started to not really care. My dad always seemed to be gone at one time or another so there wasn't a lot of stability in our house. When my dad was around there was a constant overshadowing fear in our house, shared by my sister and myself, that would affect us for the rest of our lives in so many ways, and that now is a source of strength for me. If it wasn't for my sister's love and protection, my life would've been completely empty and full of fear. I was in an unfamiliar world and my sister was the kind of protective and nurturing sister brothers could only dream about. There would be the normal bantering between brothers and sisters, but my sister had a higher purpose in this world and her first assignment was to watch over me, including taking punishments for me from time to time. My sister was put in this world by God to protect young children, and it started with me, her younger brother of one year. She would become a protector for young children, a truth she would manifest later on in her life when she became a defender of young abused children, and by raising three incredible and talented children of her own. She was not only an angel on Earth to me, but she is a living angel to so many young children in this world.

Once our parents divorced for the first time, my sister and I were watched over by many different babysitters. My mom, like so many other single mothers, had to work swing or late shifts while being challenged to get to and from work as a single mom. My sister and I knew and understood that Mom had to go to work, but we still felt alone on a daily basis, being shuttled from one babysitter to the next, and not seeing our precious mom till late hours of the night. These were hard lonely times for my sister and me, but thank God we had each other at all times, which to me was an incredible saving grace. We always had the hope of being together soon with our mom. I learned at an early age how incredibly powerful hope can be and would become in my life.

My mom was the most incredible, loving mother. She never left my sister and me, unless she had to work to support us, while we were young children. She was and still is the type of person that never missed a day of work, but more importantly, she never missed a day of being a great mom in every way, and I thank God for every moment of her love. She has been an inspiration in my life and I'm so thankful that God blessed me with her love and her kindness throughout my life to this day. This is one of the greatest miracles and gifts that God gave me, a loving mother like I was blessed to have. Thank you so much mom.

There were times when my sister and I would be at a babysitter's house, locked in the basement together. We would hold onto each other in the dark, cold, damp basement that seemed to be an out of sort place to be in, even with our harsh upbringing. As we would lie on a mattress on the floor, hoping for mom to pick us up as quickly as possible, we could still smell the strong stench of urine from some of the other children that were being watched there at different times. We were told to sleep on those mattresses, and in that cold locked basement which reminded me of a dungeon in a big castle. It was frightening, but God loved and protected us during those long and lonely nights. God was again watching over me and never left me with His never ending love.

I can still remember when the time would come for my mom to come and pick us up. It was pure joy and excitement when mom would walk through the doors and save us from the loneliness and neglect, and from what I understand now to be a form of abuse. Even though I was barely awake, I could hardly wait to be held by my mom one more time. These were the victories of my everyday life as a child, and little did I realize that my sister and I were being held in Jesus Christ's arms the entire time, and were always being protected by our Father in heaven. This is what I know and believe.

As my sister and I got a little older, we soon realized that our young lives would be a lot of macaroni and cheese dinners, and an occasional Friday night happy meal, but would mostly involve spending time with our mom, who was always there for us, no matter what, unless she was at work. To me this was just fine as long as we were all together. We would settle into a little house in a small town in southern California and we just learned how to survive as kids, and as a family.

I was always challenged at school as a young boy, and I wasn't attentive enough to be able to succeed in the public school system. My main challenge in elementary school was reading. I guess, at that point, I had no motivation to do any better, as I was just trying to survive in my life. I would often find myself in the principal's office for one thing or another, and was also always being tutored as a second and third grader because I couldn't read very well. The truth is that I was always being helped in one way or another, and I didn't realize how blessed I was at the time, but I was. I felt, for the most part, very isolated as I didn't have any friends. My mom, and sister, and our fun sheep dog named Rufus made up our small family unit, but I felt very isolated and was mostly in a constant state of fear and anxiety about what would happen next.

I love remembering the happier times of my childhood, like when my sister and I would come home from school and see the front window broken by 'you know who'- that's right, our dog Rufus would find a way to escape from our little white house. He was a strapping young sheep dog who would look for ways to create trouble, and he normally was successful. Of course, my sister and I would be summoned by my mom to go find the dog, and bring him home. Sometimes, that activity of finding our dog would take us to what seemed like faraway places around the neighborhood, but we would always end up locating the dog, although the real problem we had was catching him, which was a tall order in itself. If Rufus was born a football running back, he would've been the number one draft pick. Rufus had moves that could fake anyone out, especially two young kids. Now that was fun for my sister and me, but never easy. However, we always seemed to make it home just in time for dinner and that was a good thing. The family was together again and that made me as happy as ever.

As time went on, I found myself getting into trouble in the neighborhood even more, as 7 and 8 year old(s) sometimes do. I started to drift farther and farther from home without realizing how dangerous it truly was. I was being protected by God again, without realizing it, as my sister and I did not have the knowledge of Jesus Christ at this point in our lives. It was actually a phase of stability in my life, as I now had a full time babysitter who lived just a couple houses from us, so no more sleeping in the dungeon. Our new babysitter was a warm and caring person who had two sons. They were very nice to us and made us feel like part of their family. She would always feed us and make us do our homework and then make us brush our teeth. She truly cared for us in every way possible.

One of the sons played drums in a band, and the other was a fine athlete, and this caught my eye. I would love to just watch the son play those drums for what seemed like hours, or watch the other play baseball and football. I didn't realize at the time, but drums would change my life in the future years, in so many ways, and add so much purpose to my life. God actually had it in His purpose for me in the future. In fact, drums are still a big part of my life even as I get older and continue to play in bands, including my church's worship band which is a gift to my life.

My mom started to get more longevity and stability with her company and was getting regular hours at work, so things seemed more stable for me than ever before in my life. I was still having issues at school, but was starting to catch up with my classmates in regards to being able to read and doing math, but most importantly, I was starting to learn how to have a little bit of fun. I was still challenged and seemed to be always daydreaming and thinking about other things. I truly had some serious focusing problems and I wasn't very interested in learning. I had actually gotten a new best friend, and the two of us would spend every day together after school, and would sometimes spend Friday nights at each other's house for a sleepover. It was awesome to have such a close friend for the very first time in my life and I was happier than ever. Again, the Lord was watching over me in my young life without me even being aware of Him.

One day my mom sat my sister and me down to let us know that our father would be coming to pick us up to visit and show us the place where we will be moving to. It seems they had decided to get back together and give it another try as a married couple. For most kids this would have been great news, but I was very sad and confused as I had just started to settle into my life and was not ready to move 100 miles away to San Diego. I wasn't very close to my dad at all at that time. My dad was always leaving for some reason or another, even when my mom and father were together. I never really knew why, but I always noticed that my mom was happier when my father was gone. Now, my father was coming back into our lives and this seemed like bad news because I was unsure of how we would be treated. When I was younger, I didn't fully realize the importance of having my father back in my life again. My sister and I had started to do things in our lives that could have pointed us in a bad direction, so the prospects of having a father who cared about our well-being weren't all bad. But, to me, it just meant another big change and more instability in my life. Even though I didn't realize it at the time, this would be a major turning point in my life for so many reasons, and I now know that God was in complete control of my life when this was all happening.

As I look back at my life, I realize that I did not know about God until I was about 10 years old. As I grew older, I had to come to grips with many of my abandonment issues regarding my father, who was generally not around until I was 7 years old. This had a big impact on me as a young boy. Unfortunately, many people have to face many issues from when they were young children. I can honestly say that the only way I was able to fully heal from all my issues was through my faith in Jesus Christ, and the fact that God, Jesus, and the Holy Spirit have never abandoned me, and never will. Jesus has always been faithful and will always be through His grace.

As humans on Earth we are born into sin and we all fall short, but thankfully by believing in Jesus Christ we receive grace, a gift from

God that came at a serious cost to His Son Jesus Christ. If we receive it, we will be given the ability and the strength to walk in God's truth in our lives through Jesus Christ. When I accepted Jesus into my heart, God gave me grace, and through time, the Holy Spirit healed me, and God's grace gave me the ability to forgive my father for not being there for me in so many ways when I was a young child.

We have access to our Father in heaven by grace through Jesus Christ, and we are justified by His grace when we accept Jesus as our Lord and Savior. Romans 5:2-5 states, "Through him we have also obtained access by faith into this grace in which we stand, and we rejoice in hope of the glory of God. More than that, we rejoice in our sufferings, knowing that suffering produces endurance, and endurance produces character, and character produces hope, and hope does not put us to shame, because God's love has been poured into our hearts through the Holy Spirit who has been given to us."

So off we went to another new town, and a new place to live, where we would all be together again. I thought that as long as I had my sister and my mom I would be happy, regardless of where we lived, or if my father would stay or not. The city we moved to was actually a very nice place to live in and still brings fond memories to this day. But the first few months were a hard transition for me to make. In the new school, as a 3rd grader, I found it to be very difficult, and I was actually very lonely as I didn't make any friends at all. It was difficult to have a close friend as I started to drift into my own little world again and being on my own all the time. I would watch all the other kids play as I stayed by myself without interacting with them. This was another lonely phase for me in my young life. But what I didn't realize at the time was that I was once again being protected and watched over by God without knowing it. I was exactly where God wanted me to be, and He was strengthening me even as a young boy.

With the family all together and starting over, my father decided to have our family go to a Catholic Church for the first time in my life. I remember to this day how much I loved going to church. I would put the family's money in the offering basket when it came by. I thought this was really fun and, in time, I decided to serve the church and become an altar boy. During this time I would attend the 'Tuesday night youth Bible studies' and learn more about Jesus, the Father, and the Holy Spirit. I would enjoy these times with the other young kids, and I started to come out of my shell one day at a time for the very first time in my life. I loved being an altar boy as I got to assist the priest during different types of church services, including funerals and all the holiday services.

I didn't realize it at the time, but God had started giving me an understanding about Jesus' life on Earth, what that meant for all people, and what faith was truly all about. I loved these times in my life as the Lord was starting to work in my heart and was bringing peace to my young heart without me even realizing it. Jesus was giving me His peace, and I was receiving it. Sometimes, when I look back at my life, I am amazed at the love that I received from our Father in heaven, and our Lord and Savior Jesus Christ, and how God has always been faithful to me in guiding me through the path of my life.

When I reached the 6th grade, I went to a new school where I met my new best friend. We immediately became best buddies due to the fact that both of us loved to play baseball, basketball, and every other sport we could get our hands on. My new friend would be my first real friend in 4 years since I moved to San Diego. I was so excited to spend time with my friend. Every day we would be in class together, then we would play sports till each of us had to go in for the night. His family actually moved into my neighborhood in the 6th grade which was so cool. This was a great time for me, and we continued to be friends for many years to come. I had been blessed again with a new friend, and we are friends even to this day, even though we live on different sides of the country, we still talk from time to time. God had watched over and blessed me again through a new friendship without me even realizing it.

Life was finally on a good path for me as my family was together, even though there was a serious disconnection between my father and me. I could sometimes feel the tension between my mom and dad as well, yet they continued to stay together for the family's sake. At the time, I did not appreciate that staying together was such a gift and blessing until later on in my life. Even though my father was still very strict and not very open with his feelings towards me, I was starting to notice that I was actually important to my dad and that he loved me. I started to make it a point to give my dad a hug every night, no matter what. It was usually one of the best times of my day, as my dad started to become more expressive towards me, even if for just a minute. I truly believe that us going to church as a family had a direct correlation on how my relationship with my father was starting to heal. I saw how God was working in my life, and I truly believe that God was working in my father's life as well. This was a true turning point in my life.

I was starting to grow into a young man and I became very athletic. This was also the time when my father and I started spending more time together. We would play catch in the back yard with a baseball or football, and we would also play basketball together. This was also a time when I started to see some positive results for myself in school for the first time in life. I was starting to go to a local youth gathering called 'Young Life' where we would talk about Jesus Christ and just spend time together. Even though I had been a part of the Catholic Church and was an altar boy, I didn't yet have the same type of relationship with Jesus Christ as I do today. I was extremely interested in God and wanted to be with young people who seemed to care about others. I felt wanted and embraced, and now that I look back on it, I really needed to feel that way. I was craving to be loved. God was blessing me only in the way God can, with patience and gentleness, kindness, love, and sometimes with discipline. In His time God was bringing me up and nurturing me into His purpose and truth for me in Christ.

Let me share a story that I haven't shared with too many people, about a life changing experience when I was a young teenager. I will call this my *miracle #2*. Every once in a while, on Saturday's, my father and I would go to the beach and spend some time together. I look back at those times and I will always cherish them when it comes to our relationship. There was one day in particular that was very overcast in the morning, and I had just gotten a body board to ride some waves. It didn't have a leash to protect me from losing the board if a big wave hit me. This would almost prove to be the reason that would potentially end my life. I was an average swimmer, definitely not the type of swimmer I needed to be to handle a strong rip current that was on the beach that day. I had never learned how to navigate out of a rip current. It is done by swimming with the current and not against the current. I was in the ocean having fun on the waves and my father was on the beach with no lifeguard on duty. I can still see the wave that I was riding as I fell off it, and lost my board, and got caught in some white wash. I kept trying to swim to the shore, but was only going farther out into the ocean, and I was starting to really get tired. In fact, I was almost out of energy and was yelling for help but couldn't see anybody. I was getting scared as I was all by myself, or at least that's what I thought. God was with me, and at that very moment, God sent an angel to save my life. I believe that God has assigned angels for all of us. In my heart I believe that we are all protected in Christ supernaturally at times.

Just as I thought I was starting to go under, out of nowhere a surfer picked me out of the water and put me on his surf board. He told me to ride it all the way into the beach. As I made it to the beach, my life was saved. But the amazing thing was that I looked and there was no surfer to be found in the water. I ran to tell my father what had happened, and we looked for the board and the surfer, and they were both gone. I know in my spirit that an angel had been dispatched by God to save me that day. This was another miracle in my life. The reason I love to share these miracles is that some people are always looking for miracles, but they can't seem to find any. I am living proof of how God has worked many miracles in people's lives. I truly believe we are all miracles if we look deep enough around the gift of life. Miracles are everywhere around us right now. We can all see a true miracle of life if we just look in the mirror.

I realize now that our Lord and Savior Jesus Christ had come to this world over 2000 years ago to save all of us, through His blood, for the redemption of our sins. If you want a miracle in your life, just look to Jesus and you will find a miracle of grace (unmerited favor) for all those who believe. I had been saved on the beach that day, but the biggest gift of all is to be saved for eternity through grace and mercy in Jesus Christ. *I believe!!!*

CHAPTER 2

My Adolescence
(God's Path for Me)

My life was basically normal in high school and as a young man I truly enjoyed competing in athletics. These activities helped me in making more friends, and some of these friends made a big impact on my young life. I also had some coaches that had a big impact on my life, especially my golf coach who truly loved Jesus Christ. He obviously lived the life of someone who was saved. My coach was a great example of how a man could live so as to have a profound effect on young men like me. I remember how important core values like integrity, honesty, and his treatment of people with the highest respect, honor, and courtesy, were to him. He was an important part of my life, even though at the time I didn't realize it. Most young people do not fully comprehend just how a person can impact their lives until later on in life. I was given a great example of a man living a godly life, but at that time I didn't understand how it could have such a profound effect on my future life. God had continually shown me why he was a part of my life before I even realized it, and his significance as a role model for me.

As I look back in time and look at the impact some of my coaches have made in my life, I can truthfully say that God was always preparing me to become some type of coach. In so many ways, part of my life has been molded in Christ. Today I coach high school basketball at a local high school, and I have been coaching young men and girls for 18 years now. I thank God everyday for the opportunity to be a light and a positive reflection in the lives of young people, just like my coaches were for me. As I coach, I encourage strong core values like teamwork, family, hard work, maximum effort, doing your best, integrity, honesty, and self-belief, and also on always staying positive no matter what. I always take the opportunity to share the truth about my life and my faith walk, and how it could potentially affect their walk. Being with young people keeps me young, and I know it's an important part of my truth and life in Christ, and I'm thankful that I'm walking in it.

This can be a prime example of what living our truth in Christ is all about. Caring and giving back and being a light in Christ to others.

As I was finishing high school, I didn't realize that I had avoided a lot of the pitfalls that some teenagers go through during their four years of high school. I wasn't part of the party scene and always stayed involved in school athletics which used up a majority of my time, instead of getting caught up in activities that weren't good for me. Having a very strict father, who would not allow certain types of activities, was a tremendous blessing for me, even though I didn't appreciate it at the time. Thanks Mom and Dad. Certain minimum standards had to be maintained in our house in order to participate in high school athletics. At the time, it seemed a bit too much to me. I was not allowed to go to some high school rituals, like parties, but looking back, I can see that it was a blessing. Not to say that I never got into any type of trouble, but the level of problems was not exasperated by the element of partying and heavy relationships that can be present in those environments. God, once more, was watching over me. At the time I remained unaware of just how much God was guiding my life for His glory and purpose for me.

After I graduated, I began turning into a young man and more of the world was coming at me in so many different ways; I was changing and starting to make different choices. My father and mother had finally decided to end their marriage for the final time. The family would now be separated for good, but it all seemed fine at this point. My sister was already off to college, so it was just me and my mom. I had decided to not go to a four year college, and went to a junior college instead, so I could stay close to home, my mom, and my friends. It was a time of growth and exploration for me as tried many new things. I had decided to go to a school nearby, and in my first year of college I had excellent focus. I worked very hard and achieved good grades, but I began to do what a lot of young men do at this time in their lives. I started to experience the fun of spending more and more time with girls and going to parties. I started participating in the kind of behavior that could've lead me down a path of no return. This was the beginning of an exciting new life for me. I had not really been able, in my younger days, to go out and do what I wanted to do, whenever I wanted to do it until this point in my life. I was definitely starting to do just that, without much regard for what it would do to my future. I was enjoying having no real restrictions for the first time in my life.

I experienced some changes in my second year in school as I found other opportunities that would distract me from my studies. It was the prospect of making money. I had held jobs before but never thought about making a lot of money selling products as a salesman. I was quite good at speaking in front of and motivating audiences even at a young age, and seemed to thrive in this type of environment. As this progressed, my studies suffered, which eventually resulted in me dropping out of college. A decision I regretted, but never rectified, as life seems to have a way of moving forward not backwards. I was beginning to put myself in situations of debt and feeling a burden of financial responsibilities. I had placed myself in certain situations to try to fit into an image of success by buying a sports car to look more successful than I actually was. I was beginning to conform by creating an image of myself in the world. I didn't realize or understand that I was going down this road.

My Miracle Story #3

One night on a winding road, I was driving my new sports car that I had just purchased. I was driving very fast, but I felt in total control despite going through a series of windy turns. The car started to lose control, spinning 360 degrees and going about 80 miles per hour. That's right; I was totally out of control in my brand new sports car. Now that I look back at it, from a bigger perspective, it was parallel to how I was living my life in that moment. I was completely out of control in almost every aspect of my life. But by the grace of God, He took over the wheel and it seemed like I was in slow motion in the car. I actually looked to the side of me as I was spinning. God brought me back under control, without stopping or hitting any number of trees that were lining each side of the road.

It was a huge blessing that there were no other cars coming towards me. I now know that I was in His grace and protection once again. God had saved my life in a miracle again. Although it seemed like I was in slow motion as I was spinning through this curve, this event actually happened very fast. Every time I think about it, I get the chills. It was obviously a gift from heaven that my life was spared again. I could've easily ended up wrapped up in a tree. Thank you Jesus Christ and our Father in heaven for saving me again. My life started progressing down a different path. I was now going down a sinful path. I had now stopped going to the church and had started experimenting with negative things in my life. I was seeing multiple girls and I was spending money above my means. I started to use credit just to fit in. I started making decisions for my future that were not based on reality. In retrospect, this path actually led me to my true purpose. It's amazing how God works through phases of our life that may seem out of control to us, but is right where He wants us to be. God's sovereignty is almighty and hard to comprehend, but in my heart, I believe that God allowed me to walk down this chosen path and guided me through it to be where I am today.

I think if we all look back at our lives and see the path that we've taken, a lot of these paths may seem like tremendous mistakes, but they have all guided His chosen children to where they are today for His glory. Our true purpose in Christ comes from all of our paths, as that's the testimony we can share with others. God is amazing. God works in everything. No matter what path we take, God is working within that path for what is best for us, and His true purpose will shine through us for His glory. Stay thankful, hopeful, faithful, and patient as God is working in all your paths. God is sovereign and I believe He is always running after us. As I looked back at this season of my life, I realized that during this time I was losing touch with my friends and family, and started to develop relationships with others who weren't necessarily beneficial or positive for my life. I felt trapped, like most of us do at some point in our lives, as my decisions became more and more significant to my life. I couldn't find that peaceful place in my life. I was circling the well and I wasn't able to find a way out on my own. All of a sudden I felt lost and out of touch inside my heart, and started to withdraw from others.

As I grew older, my life got based on survival and having a good time. Time was starting to fly by and I felt like whatever chance I had of doing what was in my heart was gone now. I was under a mountain of sin and debt, and couldn't seem to find my way out of it. At this point in my life, I had reached a crossroad where most people eventually get to during their lives. I thought what do I do now? Where will I get my answers from? Who or what will help me? I was scared and didn't know what do to. Have any of you ever felt this way?

Time would go by and a lot of people would come into my life because of the decisions that I made to create a life for myself and to be able to take care of myself. These decisions at the time seemed unfavorable to me but they were things I thought I needed to do to succeed. At this point in my young life, I decided to get away from everything and everyone and join the United States Air Force. Wow, what a cultural shock that was. Looking back now, it was a true blessing because of the people that would come into my life at that point in my life. Remember, God is sovereign and wants to be a part of our lives, no matter where we are.

One thing that serving my country did for me was that it snapped me back into reality in as far as I became a person who was now more responsible. It reinforced the truth about teamwork and what it meant to be dependable. It gave me structure, discipline, and the stability that I needed, plus still allowed me to make my own decisions and be independent. I sometimes still fought the idea of structure while I was in the service, but when I think about the friendships I was blessed with during active duty it brings a smile to my face. There were so many incredible individuals that took me in and made me part of their family. All my young life I truly desired to be a part of something special. God did this for me, as He put me on this path. It gave me sense of belonging that I desperately craved. This time in my life was a turning point in so many ways.

While I was in the service, I made some powerful friendships including a young man who played the guitar and grew up in a country atmosphere. We instantly became good friends and we loved playing music together. I would eventually move to his family's country home outside of Denver, Colorado. It was a place that God used to allow me to truly find myself. There was a peaceful isolation during winters when it would snow. Though part of me felt stranded again, I actually loved it. This showed me that I had started to find some peace within myself. The most special thing this friend did for me was sharing the 'Gospel of Jesus Christ' and inviting me to his church for service and dinner. They were all loving and kind people, and they really opened up their church and showed me what a Christian church family is all about: being loving, gentle, kind, patient, and gracious towards others. Being with other Christians is special and different from the normal world. It is God's gift of a heavenly family, and I experienced it for the first time in my life.

I started playing the drums more and more, while being in the service, with a number of little bands and enjoyed how it felt. When I was visiting my friend's church one day, their worship drummer couldn't make it and so the pastor himself came to me and asked me to play drums with the worship team, even though I had never rehearsed the songs or ever even played worship music. What a blessing that turned out to be, in so many ways, but mostly because God's providence and grace gave me the gift of dwelling in Christ's worship for the first time. Playing drums in worship to my Savior has become a big part of my life today, as part of my truth and purpose in Jesus Christ. I currently play with the worship band at my church and have done so for many years now. It is one of the things I love most about my life; to be able to worship and be an instrument for God. I will share more on that later.

The next huge miracle in my life, because of the decision to go into the United States Air Force, was a person God brought into my life. She was God's true gift to me, a young lady that would later become my partner in life, as my wife and mother of our two children Luke and Mariah. I was introduced to Rori through someone I had met while I was in the service. I would have never met my beautiful wife, and had these incredible children, if I had not made the decision to join the service. God's sovereignty shows itself in God's time, not in our time, which is the beauty of God's truth in our lives. When we follow a path that is actually intended for good by God in His purpose, it will lead continually into our truth in Christ for His Glory. God is Almighty.

CHAPTER 3

Step off the Fence of this Life and Into Everlasting Life (Be Saved In Christ)

Revelations 3:15, 16 states, "I know your works: you are neither cold nor hot. Would that you were either cold or hot! So, because you are lukewarm, and neither hot nor cold, I will spit you out of my mouth." Jesus Christ is telling us not to live in this place of separation from Him. He is showing us that this place of lukewarm, or in the middle and on the fence, is a place that is worse off than any other place we can put ourselves in our lives. Although this truth can dwell in different areas of our lives, with most of us at different seasons in our lives, we don't have to choose to stay in this dark place anymore. We can decide to fully devote ourselves to God and Jesus Christ and the truth of the Gospel, and to the path that Jesus Christ has put forth in His true divine purpose for us.

Mark 8:33, "Set our minds on the things of God, not on the things of man." God wants us to ultimately submit our thoughts and lives to

Jesus Christ and to believe in the truth of the Word of God. The "things of God" are in the gospel, and God wants us to look to Jesus Christ, moment by moment, in everything we do in our lives, and to do His will even when the work is difficult and the future looks bleak. God wants 100% of us, not 50%, and our Father in heaven is there for us at every step of our lives. God wants us to trust in Him all the time, not just some of the time. Trust God. He loves you.

When our appointed time comes, and we repent for all of our sins, and make a choice to accept Jesus Christ into our life as our Lord and Savior, we are at that point "a new creation in Christ." Amen. We are *born again* and we no longer belong to this world and are no longer a slave to sin, and we belong to Jesus Christ.

Jesus is now our Lord and Savior, our brother, friend, and we are saved and forgiven of all our trespasses from the past, present, and future. John 3:16 states, "For God so loved the world, that he gave his only Son, that whoever believes in him should not perish but have eternal life." This scripture is the greatest gift and blessing to mankind, but it doesn't have to stop there. I believe that one of God's purposes is for us to glorify Him in our lives every day, on a moment by moment basis, to fulfill His purpose for us. Praise God for His amazing grace that is overflowing into us through His Son Jesus Christ and through the Holy Spirit. The Lord has plans for us right now, not to just wait to be glorified when we pass to the next life, but in our daily lives every day. 1 Peter 1:13 states, "Therefore, preparing your minds for action, and being sober-minded, set your hope fully on the grace that will be brought to you at the revelation of Jesus Christ."

God wants us to shine like a lamp that stands in the hope of Jesus Christ so that everyone who sees the believer will see this hope in them and that they are not of this world, but are dwelling in Christ. 2 Corinthians

2:14 tells us, "But thanks be to God who in Christ always leads us in triumph as trophies of Christ's victory and through us spreads and makes evident the fragrance of the knowledge of God everywhere." God's fragrance is the way we live our lives and how we love others, and most importantly, how we love and trust God right now, in everything that has to do with our lives. I encourage everybody to step off the fence of this life and into everlasting life and believe in Jesus Christ as your Lord and Savior.

I believe that God is calling you right now to become His child if you haven't already received Jesus Christ as your Lord and Savior. This could be your time to become a true child of God in His Son Jesus Christ. I pray it's your time to answer His call for you. That's right. Right now can be your time if you are ready to become a 'born again Christian.' This can be your moment of choice to become a new creation in Christ.

The Call to Everlasting Life

***This will be the biggest and most important moment in your life, and I believe it's the most important choice any person can ever make while alive in this world, while desiring an everlasting life, and while living with true purpose. I pray you take this step before moving on with the rest of the book.

Don't look back. Move forward into your calling of faith in Christ Jesus and live and walk in your truth in Christ through His grace. Step off the fence once and for all and into Christ and His righteousness, and be saved for eternity.

You can ask Jesus to be your Lord and Savior right this very moment wherever you are.

Just ask the Lord Jesus Christ for forgiveness of your sins and repent for your life of sin, and speak out loud that you believe that Jesus Christ has died for your sins, and that you believe your sins will be forgiven through the blood of Jesus Christ, and that you now accept Jesus Christ into your heart and life as your Lord and Savior through faith in Jesus Christ.

***If you have done this you are now saved in Christ Jesus. You are now a 'born again Christian,' a believer, a saint, and a new creature in Christ. ***

Jesus says in Luke 15:7, "Just so, I tell you, there will be more joy in heaven over one sinner who repents than over ninety-nine righteous persons who need no repentance." If you have taken this call and have become 'born again in Christ,' then in heaven there is much joy for you. I am so thankful for Christ and His love for us. Walk in His love my brothers and sisters. Your spirit is now cleansed by the blood of Jesus Christ forever. You are saved and redeemed in Christ.

At this point it's very important for you to find a local church where you can move forward in your walk in Christ Jesus and the Gospel of Truth. It's going to be very nourishing for you to have fellowship with other believers and to start spending time in the Holy Bible, and to speak to a Christian pastor for prayer and for Christian guidance in your new walk in Christ. You are now in Christ and will be for eternity. You are now my everlasting brother or sister in Christ. I praise Jesus Christ.

You are now In the Great I Am through grace and a new creature in Christ.

CHAPTER 4

Born Again
(Saved in Christ)

When I was almost 30 years old, I accepted Jesus Christ into my heart as my Lord and Savior and my life has never been the same since. My life slowly began to change and go in different directions. Once I became a child of God, and repented for my sins and accepted Jesus Christ into my heart, it felt like it was the perfect time to do so, now that I look back at how it all happened. God works in our lives through every moment whether we know it or not. God knew exactly where I was in my heart and how I had lived my life to that point, and He had predestined me to accept His Son Jesus Christ into my heart at that very second in time. I believe, with all my heart, that God has us on His path even when it looks like we are off the mark. God has a purpose for all paths for and to His Glory. Obviously there is a mystery in how God works, but in my heart I believe that God uses everything for good and for His purpose.

Believers immediately start to go through a process called *transformation,* a process that God works within all of us through the Holy Spirit as we become enlightened in the truth of His Word for us. In Acts 26:18 Jesus Christ tells us, "To open their eyes, so that they may turn from darkness to light and from the power of Satan to God, that they may receive forgiveness of sins and a place among those who are sanctified by faith in me." Hebrews 10:10 states, "And by that will we have been sanctified through the offering of the body of Jesus Christ once and for all." Once we accept Christ into our hearts and spirits, our spirits are immediately pure and sanctified for eternity in Christ. We are perfected forever in Christ as we are now sanctified in and through grace. Our flesh and our minds go through a period of renewal and transformation as a 'born again Christian.' I am in a state of renewing my mind and body every single day as the Holy Spirit guides me in this process and in the renewal of my mind. I sometimes still fall short, but I am not a slave to sin anymore.

Romans 6:5-11 states, "For if we have been united with him in a death like his, we shall certainly be united with him in a resurrection like his. We know that our old self was crucified with him in order that the body of sin might be brought to nothing, so that we would no longer be enslaved to sin. For one who has died has been set free from sin. Now if we have died with Christ, we believe that we will also live with him. We know that Christ, being raised from the dead, will never die again; death no longer has dominion over him. For the death he died he died to sin, once for all, but the life he lives to God. So you also must consider yourselves dead to sin and alive to God in Christ Jesus." This truth is something that all new believers will experience when they become born again, and will continue to experience for the rest of their lives until they return home to heaven and become glorified. Always remember once you are in the grace of Christ, you are righteous and sanctified in your spirit. Through the faith that God gave me I started to spend more time in His Word of Truth, and this, through the Holy Spirit, started to produce more goodness and fruits of Spirit in my life. I started abiding in the truth of Jesus Christ through grace and God's mercy for me, and I started spending more time praying to my father in Heaven instead of trying to do everything on my own. This is all to the glory of Jesus Christ as He started to impute His qualities on me as a new believer, through the Word of God and the Holy Spirit.

Looking back at my life and how I spent a tremendous amount of time rebelling and having fun in my 20's, I believe it was due to the fact that I was living in so much fear as a young boy. I spent a lot of my childhood living in the bondage and stronghold of fear and isolation in my own home. I didn't have many opportunities to have a good time and be free like a lot of children do. Although this put me on the path of sin, I believe it also put me on the path to realizing that I needed a Savior in Jesus Christ. Along the way, I grew up and became an adult and I encountered another major burden that life brought. Acquiring debt in my life would become a burden, and would dictate a lot of my decisions in my youth as I got trapped in the flesh. So often the circumstances in our lives start dictating the choices we make. We may lose track of our passions in life and the gifts that God has given us, and potentially allow these circumstances to create excuses for not following our true purpose and passions in life.

These gifts may be special gifts that God has given to us as His children, or it may be a higher purpose that we believe we want to fulfill for others. These pursuits and passions are things that stir our souls and spirits toward another level of purpose. These gifts are our true purpose that God has put forth for us in our lives, and that's why I call it the truth in my life in Christ. These gifts are generally the things that drive us the most or that we may love the most. Romans 8:29 states, "For those whom he foreknew he also predestined to be conformed to the image of his son, in order that he might be the firstborn among many brothers." This tells us that God's purpose for our lives is to be more and more like His Son Jesus, through His grace. Our true calling is to be more and more like Jesus, and for His glory to shine out of us and towards other people and to be stewards and Ambassadors for Christ.

Matthew 11:28-30 states, "Come to me, all who labor and are heavy laden, and I will give you rest. Take my yoke upon you, and learn from me, for I (Jesus) am gentle and lowly in heart, and you will find rest for your souls. For my yoke is easy, and my burden is light." This is an incredible gospel truth that I encourage all believers to remember daily as an important reality of their lives. Leave all your problems at the cross and rejoice in today and in what God wants for you, and do not to dwell on doubts, fears, and anxieties about yesterday, today, or tomorrow. This is an amazing truth and blessing that the Lord Jesus Christ has showered on all His children in Christ.

I had always lived my life in an independent way. I always felt like I had to take care of myself or nobody else would. This gospel truth resonates with me and is a big part of my walk with Christ Jesus. I was always living in the past and constantly reliving my sins and failures. Fortunately for me, the truth of the Word of God wants believers to dwell in the truth that our sins are forgiven, and we are justified in Christ Jesus from now and forever. We must believe this truth to have peace. Our forgiveness and righteousness has nothing to do with us, but has everything to do with the righteousness of Jesus Christ and His grace. Jesus is our righteousness.

Responsibility in life will sneak into our lives without us knowing it and as a young adult that was the case for me. We all know this type of growth will come into our lives once we start down the path of adulthood. For some it's the responsibility of student loans when embarking on college. For others, it's the responsibility of being in a young relationship and having children at a young age.

There is a tremendous amount of stress that can be added to the life of a young adult once they leave their home and start to make decisions on their own. Life comes at all of us in so many ways and in different forms. Responsibility is something that a lot of young adults just aren't ready for, but it's a big part of growing up. Accepting it and doing the best you can to deal with responsibility is a quality that God wants us to acquire through faith and trust in Him. The truth is we can't do it on our own, the way God wants us to do it; we need to trust that God will, and is bringing us down the path that He wants us to be on, and that he has already blessed us in every way. Trust that God is sovereign in your life, always has been, and always will be. God will work in all parts of your life no matter where you are.

When I was a young man I had decided to buy a nice car for myself and trade the car that was paid for to present a different image of myself to people than what the truth was. I was caught up in trying to create an image of myself in front of others that wasn't truly accurate, so I could be someone I wasn't. Sound familiar? I used to believe in the old adage "fake it till you make it." You see, I had gone into the sales business and was constantly looking for that perfect product or big sale. I thought that I needed to be someone successful very fast. I was always trying to get there a little faster than the next guy, and I was missing out on the fun of the journey. Sometimes, in life, we get lost and we feel we can't find our way back to that place of peace or our true purpose. This was the case for me before I found the Lord. I was constantly searching for answers and never seemed to find peace with where I was at that moment. Have any of you ever been unsettled in your lives or are you unsettled right now? What I didn't realize at the time was I couldn't see the amazing blessings and grace that God was pouring on me on a daily basis, even before I had accepted Jesus Christ as my Lord and Savior. God had been blessing me in so many ways which included bringing me a beautiful girlfriend who would become my future wife and the mother of my two children. I wasn't able to see that far ahead.

God is completely sovereign, even when we perceive our lives are crumbling and falling apart. God is and has always been, working in every situation for His Glory and for the betterment of our lives, regardless of the paths we choose to take. All good comes from God, but I believe that He works the good out of anything, good or bad. This is God's sovereignty in our lives. Ultimately God works in every aspect of our lives for the purpose of His glory, even the terrible stuff although nothing bad comes from God. That is my true testimony that I can offer to anyone; God has brought me through all of the strongholds in my life and brought me victory through Jesus Christ.

God knows exactly what we need and what we don't need. God hears all our prayers before we even pray them. God had already put my life on the eternal right track when he predestined me and you for adoption through the blood of Jesus Christ. Ephesians 1:4-12 states, "Even as he chose us in him before the foundation of the world, that we should be holy and blameless before him. In love he predestined us for adoption as sons through Jesus Christ according to the purpose of his will, to the praise of his glorious grace, with which he has blessed us in the Beloved. In him, we have redemption through his blood, the forgiveness of our trespasses, according to the riches of his grace, which he lavished upon us, in all wisdom and insight making known to us the mystery of his will, according to his purpose, which he set forth in Christ as a plan for the fullness of time, to unite all things in him, things in heaven and things on earth. In him we have obtained an inheritance, having been predestined according to the purpose of him who works all things according to the counsel of his will, so that we who were the first to hope in Christ might be to the praise of his glory."

I had accepted Jesus Christ as my Lord and Savior at a time in my life when I was out of control and lost. The Lord through grace and the blood of Jesus had put a measure of faith into my heart, and when the call came to me to become part of the family of God through faith in Jesus Christ, I heard and "believed." That very second, I had jumped off the fence and into grace forever. I was forgiven, and now a child of God, and was now purchased by the blood of Jesus Christ for all time. Romans 8:15-17 states, "For you did not receive the spirit of slavery to fall back into fear, but you have received the Spirit of Adoption as sons, by whom we cry, "Abba! Father!" The Spirit himself bears witness with our spirit that we are children of God and if children, then heirs."

What exactly does this mean? It means that God chose us, who believe in Christ Jesus as our Lord and Savior, before the world had even started. That we should be holy and blameless before Him, only because of God's grace and love for us, not because of anything that we have done or will ever do, but by everything Jesus Christ has done by taking my punishment for my sins as a propitiation. It was God's will for this to happen. God had shown me the mystery of His will, and what He wanted to happen in my life and for those who believe in His Son Jesus Christ. Those who believe in Christ have an inheritance in heaven and in this life, and it has already been provided to us. So, *receive it*. We are to praise His glory and be a light for others, and to glorify God in everything we do. Being born again through repentance and believing in Jesus Christ as our Lord and Savior is the foundation to our "truth in Christ for Christ." God says to believe!!! Step off the fence of this life and into everlasting life in Christ Jesus and live your life *In* the *Great I Am.*

CHAPTER 5

Put On Your Armor

Ephesians 6:13-18 tells us, "Therefore take up the whole armor of God, that you may be able to withstand in the evil day, and having done all, to stand firm. Stand therefore having fastened on the belt of truth, and having put on the breastplate of righteousness, and, as shoes for your feet, having put on the readiness given by the gospel of peace. In all circumstances take up the shield of faith, with which you can extinguish all the flaming darts of the evil one; and take the helmet of salvation, and the sword of the Spirit, which is the word of God, praying at all times in the Spirit, with all prayer and supplication. To that end keep alert with all perseverance, making supplication for all the saints." Let's take a further look into these Gospel truths and gain a deeper understanding about their application in our lives, and why they are so important for a 'born again Christian.' I didn't realize how I had come to this place of belief in the gospel of Jesus Christ. I had definitely felt that I lacked in belief or faith in myself when I had become a born again Christian. So how did I come to this place of belief in Jesus Christ?

Through the gift of grace activated by faith, God works in our lives for His glory in so many different ways, and sometimes will bring us to a place of despair, or even complete joy before we can actually hear and listen to God. It doesn't always happen this way, but this is the way in which it happened for me. After a friend of mine had shared the truth about salvation and the gift of grace with me, he invited me to a mega church in Los Angeles, California. I felt like it was time to go back to church and hear the Word of God from a strong evangelist, but what I didn't realize was that I was actually being led by the Holy Spirit to be there in that very moment. Again, it's important to mention that God will always allow freedom of choice in our lives. God is sovereign in everything and knows exactly what is best for us, but God will always give us the ability to choose and make our own choices. We have to make the choice to believe, which I believe activates faith. Even when we are sinning and constantly falling short, God is working during those times of our lives, and will work everything for His perfection and glory. It's absolutely amazing.

I had finally reached that place where I "heard" the Word of Truth, not for the first time in my life, but it was 'God's perfect time' for me to come to that place of choice to repent for my sins, and accept Jesus as Lord and Savior into my life, as Romans 10:17 states, "Faith comes from hearing, and hearing through the word of Christ." I finally realized that I was a sinner and couldn't do it alone anymore, and in fact, I didn't want to do it alone. The truth is that God has always been faithful to me and has never left me, but I hadn't been faithful to God. I needed a Savior who is and has always been faithful to God, to be able to walk in righteousness through the blood of Jesus Christ, and not live in despair and be a slave to sin anymore. God had aligned the time of my life on Earth with the time that my new life would become eternal in Jesus Christ. I believe God's sovereignty is always working in everyone's life including the non-believer and the believer. This is absolutely incredible and magnificent. It is God's perfection and majesty at work in our lives, moment by moment.

So what exactly is faith according to the Word of God? Hebrews 11:1-3 states that "Now faith is the assurance of things hoped for, the conviction of things not seen. For by it the people of old received their commendation. By faith we understand that the universe was created by the word of God, so that what is seen was not made out of things that are visible." My faith in Jesus Christ as my Lord and Savior is now assured, and I believe He died for my sins and was resurrected on the third day. Jesus Christ is my Lord.

Before being saved my life didn't have a lot of meaning in my eyes, and in fact, I felt like I was going from one mistake to another, job to job, and from one relationship to another, just drifting through life. My world was still out of control, but at the time I didn't realize that God had always been working in my life and was about to bring me to a point of repentance and faith, being reborn in Christ for eternity. The old self in me was about to pass away. God would be giving me a measure of faith to believe in the Lord Jesus Christ, without me even realizing that He was working in my life again. His grace displayed itself to show me that it was based on nothing that I had done to deserve it. There is only one way to find out the truth about faith and where it comes from, and that is from the 'Gospel of Jesus Christ' or from a believer who has the Holy Spirit dwelling in him. Faith is the foundation and the shield of the believer as a new creature in Christ. Psalm 28: 7, 8 states, "The Lord is my strength and my shield; in him my heart trusts, and I am helped; my heart exults and with my song I give thanks to him. The Lord is the strength of his people; he is the saving refuge of his anointed."

Ephesians 6:16 states, "In all circumstances take up the shield of faith with which you can extinguish all the flaming darts of the evil one." In Christ, faith will be your shield to extinguish any and all of the challenges and strongholds that are a part of your life, and the hardships that can come your way. Without faith there is no hope of salvation and without faith it is impossible to please God. In order to move forward as a 'new believer' we will be brought to a place by God in our spirit, mind, and soul, where we know that God is protecting us in all aspects of our lives, and has already blessed us with everything we need. In our hearts we must know, embrace, and fasten this belt of truth around our lives with the measure of faith that God has given to us. Faith only comes from God, not from us, and this is an important truth we should remember moving forward in our truth in Christ. *Our choice is the belief.*

Romans 1:17 states, "The righteous shall live by faith." Righteousness as a Christian is built around Christ's righteousness through faith because it's not about what we do; it's about what Christ has already done for us. All things are possible with God when you believe. Ephesians 2: 8-10 states, "For by grace you have been saved through faith. And this is not your own doing; it is the gift of God, not a result of works, so that no one may boast for we are his workmanship, created in Christ Jesus for good works, which God prepared beforehand, that we should walk in them." Faith is a gift from God to the believer, to stand firm in as a Christian, and move forward in their walk, and to believe and trust that God is always faithful to His Word and to His children. This is such an important truth because it's essential to recognize that faith in Jesus Christ is 100% from God, and 0% from our self, so it's not earned by us and never can be, and it's completely unmerited. It's grace given to us, for those who believe, paid for by the blood of Jesus Christ. Choose to believe in your faith that you have received.

I didn't do anything to deserve this gift of salvation, as it was a gift from God; by His Grace we have been saved. Romans 5:1-5 states, "Therefore, since we have been justified by faith, we have peace with God through our Lord Jesus Christ. Through him we have also obtained access by faith into this grace in which we stand, and we rejoice in hope of the glory of God. More than that, we rejoice in our sufferings, knowing that suffering produces endurance, and endurance produces character, and character produces hope, and hope does not put us to shame, because God's love has been poured into our hearts through the Holy Spirit who has been given to us." I now have the gift of faith through Jesus Christ in my life. It is my shield that God has given to me moving forward, plus I now have God's Holy Spirit and His power in me through faith in Jesus Christ. I can now see past the circumstances of my life through discernment. I dwell in the gift of faith and move forward in my truth in Christ, and endure to the end, and walk in the purpose that God has for me. Through this endurance, my true self and the fragrance of Jesus has started to shine bright from within myself, and is now producing courage and hope in my life through Jesus Christ. God's love is pouring into my heart and is overflowing from my life into the lives of others.

This truth has set me free once and for all, especially from all the lies and deceit that had entrapped me for so many years. The armor of God has given me the belt of truth of Jesus Christ and has also brought the gospel into my life once and for all. Only believers have God's truth in their lives, which can defeat all the lies that are a part of living in this world. But believers are not of this world, they are now a part of the Kingdom of Heaven as a child of God.

1 John 5:6 states, "This is he who came by water and blood– Jesus Christ; not by the water only but by the water and the blood. And the Spirit is the one who testifies, because the Spirit is the truth." God's

words are the ultimate standard of truth as John 17:17 states as Jesus prayed to the Father, "Sanctify them in the truth; your word is truth." God's Word is the final standard of truth and I think once a believer fully walks in this truth, his walk will intensify into God's purpose. The sword of the Spirit is the Gospel or the Word of God, and it is what the believer has been given to know the Father, Jesus Christ, and the Holy Spirit more closely and intimately. Scripture gives us His truth on how to live our lives in Christ, and to take authority in our true identity in Christ with a new understanding of what God is doing in our lives. Once you have become a believer in Christ, the gospel will become the true mirror of your new life in Christ.

The Word of God is with me at all times as it is truly my sword. I am guided by the Holy Spirit to dwell in the Word of God, and the Holy Spirit gives me discernment or an understanding of the scriptures and how it applies to and within my life, my truth, and purpose in Christ. It will for you as well. No warrior would ever go into battle without his sword, and it's even more important as a believer to always have the Word of God with you at all times. It is sufficient for our lives in Christ and we should always dwell in the Word of God. Romans 15:4 states, "For whatever was written in former days was written for our instruction, that through endurance and through the encouragement of the Scriptures we might have hope." The Word of God brings hope into our lives and constantly gives encouragement to the believer. To dwell in our purpose in Christ and His truth, it's essential to always have our sword of the Spirit with us at all times. It's important to dwell in the Word daily, and feed off of God's truth for our lives. The Word of God is our belt of truth as a believer In Jesus Christ. God is faithful in everything, and He will be faithful to all His children dwelling in Jesus Christ, and in His truth of the Word of God.

Paul tell us in Colossians 3:9-10, "Do not lie to one another, seeing that you have put off the old self with its practices and have put on the new self, which is being renewed in knowledge after the image of its creator." I soon realized that as a new creation, I had a 'new nature,' my old root nature of sin died through grace. This changed how I communicated to others in every way. I trust in the truth of knowledge about my Father in heaven, my Lord Jesus Christ, and about where I truly come from, and the kingdom I now belong to; the Kingdom of Heaven. Through the Holy Spirit, the scriptures began to take hold in my life in so many positive and fruitful ways. Truthfulness had become a part of my new nature in Christ although I still sometimes fall short, but God is continually renewing my mind and flesh, to truth and honesty with others, and more notably while dealing with the truth in my own heart and mind regarding my life in Christ.

This aspect is very important as I continue to pray to my Father in heaven as I pray for discernment, about what I am to do for His purpose. I continue to pray the Holy Spirit would open my eyes to His truth for my life. I believe God wants us to be completely honest with ourselves and to Him. God wants us to share intimacy with Him in our prayers, although He already knows our hearts and spirits. God wants us to always trust Him and be intimate by being open and fully trust Him to guide and protect us through our walk. We should always dwell in His truth and love and give it to others, and not dwell in deceit and the lies of this world. As a believer our hearts will change through Jesus Christ and the Holy Spirit and we will seek to dwell in Christ through faith and believing in God's Word for our lives. Psalm 15:2 states, "Speak truth in his heart." So as we walk in our own personal truth in Christ let's fasten on the Belt of Truth in Jesus Christ and dwell in God's truth for our lives.

Galatians 2:16 states, "We have believed in Christ Jesus, in order to be justified by faith in Christ, and not by works of the law, because by works of the law shall no one be justified."

Justification is something that God does for us through faith in Jesus Christ. We obtain peace with God because of what Christ has done for us. Justification declares that the believer in Christ has no penalty for sin, including past, present and future sins. Romans 8:1 states, "There is therefore now no condemnation for those who are in Christ Jesus." It would be the opposite of condemnation. As we live our lives in Christ Jesus it's essential that we realize that we are free from condemnation once and for all, and to not live our lives or think in this manner any more.

This does not give the believer the right to sin, but it means that we are not a slave to sin anymore in Christ Jesus because we are rooted in Christ Jesus and His righteousness, not our own. Because of one man's sins, Adam, we were made sinners, and by another man's righteousness we were made justified and righteous because of what Christ has done for us already. It is done! Romans 5:19 states, "By one man's obedience many will be made righteous" and this is how we have peace with God through Jesus Christ."

God loves us so much. More than we can possibly comprehend, as He gave up His only Son Jesus Christ to die on a cross for those who believe. Can you imagine giving up your only son so wretched sinners could receive forgiveness. Think about this incredible gift from our Father in heaven and what Jesus Christ did for us. **Don't move on until you have taken in this truth once and for all. Justified in Christ Jesus is grace, and there is no condemnation in grace.**

Isaiah 61:10 states, "He has covered me with the robe of righteousness." Jesus Christ's righteousness has been given to all who believe in Him as their Lord and Savior, because of God's covenant with His Son and our faith in Christ Jesus. The righteousness of Jesus Christ has already been deposited into your account if you have received Jesus Christ as you're Lord and Savior. Apostle Paul wrote in Romans 5:17, "That we are those who received the free gift of righteousness." On our own we are sinners, but in Christ we are righteous in the sight of God. To be righteous in the eyes of God is an amazing free gift of grace from our Father in heaven through Jesus Christ. Let us all walk in His righteousness through faith in Jesus Christ once and for all. We who believe are clothed with the righteousness of Jesus Christ.

Romans 14:17-20 states, "For the kingdom of God is not a matter of eating and drinking but of righteousness and peace and joy in the Holy Spirit. Whoever thus serves Christ is acceptable to God and approved by men. So then let us pursue what makes for peace and for mutual up building." Being righteous will provide rest, peace, and joy in our lives, and through the Holy Spirit we will love people and build others up in the truth of Jesus Christ. I had been given a personal invitation from Jesus Christ, who is now, at this very moment, alive in the throne room of God in heaven, interceding on the believer's behalf at all times. I have taken the call or invitation from God to repent for my sins.

I believe in Jesus Christ as my Lord and Savior, and this free gift of grace from God saved me eternally, and through Jesus Christ I have put on my 'helmet of salvation.' To be forgiven from the past, present, and future sins, and have eternal life in heaven is the most precious gift that God, through Jesus Christ, has given to those who believe. The 'helmet of salvation' should be on us daily, as we move forward with our truth in Christ, because it makes us realize that we are saved eternally and we are here to serve Jesus Christ, and not ourselves anymore. Our truth in Christ will manifest through faith in Jesus Christ. It is not us who live anymore, but Christ who lives in and through us. *Our truth in Christ is Christ in us and through us.* This is important to remember as we move forward with our life in Christ. We are anointed in Christ to walk in Christ and His grace, and live our lives to share Christ's love with others.

Matthew 6:8 states, "Your father knows what you need before you ask him." So why then is prayer so important in our full armor of God? God wants us to have 100% faith and trust in Him, and not doubt anything that we ask of Him in His will for us. Prayer gives the believer the opportunity to communicate with God the creator in the name of our Lord and Savior Jesus Christ. Remember, as we get saved we become an adopted child of God. Christ has already blessed all those who believe in every blessing from God. All good things come from our Father in heaven, Jesus Christ and the Holy Spirit. Faith is us knowing that we can receive every blessing that has already been put in place for all those who believe. Receive, my brothers and sisters.

In Christ we are now heirs of God, and God is now our Father in heaven, so I encourage all believers to spend their time in prayer, and let God know what's in your heart, and pray, as there is ultimate power in Jesus Christ, in prayer through faith. Romans 12:12 tells us "to be constant in prayer" that God wants us to be praying at all times to Him, through Jesus Christ. Matthew 21:22 states, "Whatever you ask in prayer, you will receive, if you have faith." This is an amazing truth of the Word of God, that whatever we ask, we will receive, if we only have faith. God also tells us in Romans 6:18, "Praying at all times in the Spirit, with all prayer and supplication. To that end keep alert with all perseverance, making supplication for all the saints." Pray for your brothers and sisters in Christ. Persevere and be patient through every challenge of the days of your lives, and be encouraged to share this in prayer with our Father in heaven. Remember to always be thankful in prayer, to God in heaven through Jesus Christ, for all the blessings in your life. Our Father in heaven has created every aspect of our lives. God is fully sovereign in every part of our lives.

As I started to mature in my walk with Jesus Christ, I started to become conscious of just how much the Lord was, and has been, blessing me on a daily basis. I was starting to see for the first time in my life just how much God had always loved me, and how God had always been with me, and wanted to love me in every possible way a Father could love His son. God gave me His perfect love that would do away with fear from my life. God had now given me a love that was everlasting. In Christ, I was not in the darkness of sin and fear anymore. This revelation started to manifest itself in the truth of my life, and my truth in my purpose was starting to be revealed in my heart through the Holy Spirit.

The gospel teaches the believer to be ready, and to keep alert and persevere through all afflictions and challenges that people will go through in their lives. Prayer and the gospel, with our relationship with God, and our salvation through faith in Jesus Christ, will put us in line with God's purpose for us as His children. Be ready to discern in your mind, through the Holy Spirit, what comes from God, and what comes from the enemy and or the flesh, and stay focused and pray for the things of God to be revealed to you through the Holy Spirit. This aligns me with God's purpose for myself as God reveals, through the Holy Spirit, what is my truth in Christ. Keep alert to what God is showing you, and stay in prayer about every aspect of your life, and I shall pray that we are all guided by the Holy Spirit. Nothing in this transformation process happens because we deserve anything, but because God's grace is shining on the believer, through faith in Jesus Christ. So enjoy the journey that God has for you, and put on your 'full armor of God' in Christ Jesus, and start to dwell in your truth and life in Christ.

CHAPTER 6

The Power of Prayer

Jesus said in Luke 11:9-13, "And I tell you, ask and it will be given to you; seek, and you will find; knock, and it will be opened to you. For everyone who asks receives, and he who seeks finds, and to him who knocks, it will be opened. What father among you, if his son asks for a fish, will instead of a fish give him a serpent; or if he asks for an egg, will give him a scorpion? If you then who are evil know how to give good gifts to your children, how much more will the heavenly Father give the Holy Spirit to those who ask him!" We all need to look for answers and seek our inner most needs from God through genuine prayer, and not rely on ourselves in matters of our lives. If we ask God anything in prayer, He will answer according to His will and timing. 1 Timothy 2:5 states that "There is one God, and there is one mediator between God and men, the man Christ Jesus."

This passage tells the believer that our prayers are actually heard by God because we have a mediator, our Lord and Savior Jesus Christ. Jesus Christ works between God and ourselves, and allows those who believe to be in God's presence through Jesus Christ. We can have a relationship with our Father in heaven through prayer and faith in Jesus Christ. I believe God wants us to share all of our deepest and intimate thoughts and needs in a transparent manner, and be in a deeper fellowship with God and Jesus Christ through prayer. Our primary focus should be on Jesus at all times, not on ourselves or what we can do on our own, but what Jesus has already done for us. Our genuine confidence should be in Christ and God first, as we go through every part of our lives. I encourage everyone to be in a relationship with God first through Jesus Christ and the Holy Spirit, before we trust others or ourselves for every aspect of our lives.

Hebrews 10:19-22 tells us "Therefore, brothers, since we have confidence to enter the holy places by the blood of Jesus by the new and living way that he opened for us through the curtain, that is through his flesh, and since we have a great priest over the house of God, let us draw near with a true heart in full assurance of faith, with our hearts sprinkled clean from an evil conscience and our bodies washed with pure water." Therefore, we now can have the confidence to enter the Holy Place; the very presence of God Himself. Jesus Christ gives us the confidence and ability to approach God in prayer through Jesus himself and through the Holy Spirit. *Meditate on this truth before moving forward.*

We can now go to our creator, and pray and give thanks, and have an intimate relationship with God through Jesus Christ and the Holy Spirit. We are actually being heard by our Father, Jesus Christ, and the Holy Spirit when we pray in faith through Jesus Christ. This is a powerful truth that all believers should dwell on, and it is a gift from God through Jesus Christ, that we can have a relationship with our Father in heaven and share everything that we go through with God.

John 14:6 states, "I am the way, and the truth, and the life. No one comes to the Father except through me." This tells us that only through Jesus do we have access to God, our Father in heaven, and through Jesus is the only way to have a personal relationship with God. John 15:7 states, "If you abide in me, and my words abide in you, ask whatever you will, and it shall be done for you." It's so special to have God's words within us, especially when we pray in Christ. Stay in the Word of God daily, and walk in His truth and pray about the truth of your daily lives. It's truly an opportunity and a gift to be able to pray to God, that He would open doors for you, and truly bring you to your purpose and your truth in Christ Jesus.

John 15:8 states, "By this my Father is glorified, that you bear much fruit and so prove to be my disciples." The key to prayer is to abide in Jesus Christ and dwell in His truth, by believing through faith, while trusting and knowing in your spirit that God will answer all your prayers. In fact, the Lord has already given us so many blessings, but it is up to us, through our faith in Jesus Christ, to receive them. If you are in Christ, thank God for the blessings that He has already given to you, and say out loud that "I accept and take delivery of my blessings that God has given to me through Jesus Christ." Receive all your blessings in Christ.

Matthew 21:22 states that, "Whatever you ask in prayer, you will receive if you have faith". What exactly does this mean? Mark 11:24 also states, "Therefore I tell you, whatever you ask in prayer, believe that you have received it, and it will be yours." James 1:6-8 states, "But let him ask in faith, with no doubting, for the one who doubts is like a wave of the sea that is driven and tossed by the wind. For that person must not suppose that he will receive anything from the Lord; he is a double-minded man, unstable in all his ways." For me this means that prayer is my way of trusting my Father in heaven and my Lord and Savior, on a second by second basis, in my life for everything. My faith truly knows, and not just hopes; although hope is a great thing, faith and believing is everything. Faith is not about doubting because if we doubt then we are easily moved all over the place, which is where the enemy does his work by trying to create confusion in our minds and our lives. Every attack from the enemy starts with an attack on our faith. Remember this truth moving forward as a believer.

God wants us to know that if we pray in faith, it is past tense, meaning the prayer has already been answered before we even asked for it. God already knows our needs, but through belief and faith, there is an opening or a receiving of the blessing. Praying, and our belief, is our responsibility in our relationship with God, Jesus Christ, and the Holy Spirit. Doubt seems to have the opposite effect on our prayers and in our lives, as it can potentially create a blockage in our prayer life. Believe in your faith in Jesus Christ and your prayer life will continue to grow.

In my life I'm starting to have a deeper understanding of how the true power of prayer is touching my life in every way. I now recognize how God has always worked in my life to bring me closer to Him through Jesus Christ and the Holy Spirit. I now comprehend just how much God has loved me ever since before I was born. We are all God's creation and He loves us all. For years and years, I wasn't communicating with the Lord although God knew every thought I had before I ever even thought it. I know this is a hard concept for a lot of believers and non-believers to understand, but God wants us to trust Him at all times, and He wants to have an intimate loving relationship with His children. True obedience to God and Jesus Christ means having faith in Christ Jesus at all times no matter what. This is the calling in our lives as believers in Christ.

Prayer is how we personally communicate and trust God through Jesus Christ, and it is a powerful truth in my life as a believer, and in how I move forward with my purpose that God has set in motion for me. My truth and purpose in Christ for God's glory will manifest itself more and more as I continue to trust God in all aspects of my life, and communicate with Him through prayer. I love to pray for discernment, peace, strength, protection, and to walk in the resurrection power I have in Christ, and to walk in all the fruits of the Spirit as I live my life, as a believer in Jesus Christ. Communication is so important in every aspect of our lives, but especially in our prayers to God. We now have the free gift from our Father through grace to no longer be separated from Him in Christ. We can now have an intimate relationship with God through prayer and faith in Jesus Christ every second of our lives. We are truly never alone and through Christ we are at peace with God.

To say that you can accomplish your truth and true purpose in Christ without constant and continual prayer would be unattainable in my opinion. As believers, we must fully embrace that God is sovereign and makes all things happen in His time, and God will receive all the glory for everything that is accomplished by the believer. God wants us to know that we are not alone, and it's a blessing to be able to share our needs with God when we pray. Prayer is the definitive communication with God for the believer. Think about this truth. *Our Creator is hearing our prayers through Jesus Christ.* As I continue to mature and transform as a believer in the Word of God, and my faith moves forward in God's purpose with my walk in Jesus Christ, I am truly humbled by the truth of the Word of God and the beautiful gift of prayer in Christ Jesus. Prayer is an awe-inspiring opportunity for me to share with God my thoughts and what is in my heart, plus what is concerning me and what I'm excited about. It gives me the opportunity to pray for guidance, strength, and the power of the Holy Spirit through Jesus Christ. Prayer gives me complete assurance that I am not alone and that I am part of the kingdom of God through Jesus Christ. Through prayer, I can, as a believer in Christ Jesus through faith, rebuke thoughts or attacks in my mind in the name of Jesus Christ. Anxiousness, fear, confusing thoughts, wandering, or any type of mind binding spirit, can be rebuked through prayer. Praying in the Spirit is an essential part of being a believer in Christ Jesus. Believers have a direct line to God through Jesus Christ. The Holy Spirit will give us utterance to understand what to pray for and how to pray.

I pray that all of you will feel this assurance through prayer, and trust that God knows what's best for all of you as His children. The encouragement and peace that I feel through prayer is something that I can only describe as 'not of this world.' It's a true gift from God Himself that, through faith in Jesus Christ, I can come humbly with an attitude of thanksgiving go to God, without any blemish, unstained, and without sin through Jesus Christ. To pray and cast all my cares and burdens on Him, and share with God what's on my heart, and lay down all my worries and fears at the cross. Now this is true worship. I am so thankful for all that God, Jesus Christ, and the Holy Spirit have done for me in my life. I have an eternal hope concerning what's to come in my life and the life of my family, and to all my brothers and sisters in Christ, and for those who do not know Christ as of yet. How about the fact that God gave me life, that's a miracle in itself. Think about the miracle of life for a moment. It wasn't an accident. Life is a purposeful gift from God.

Just look in the mirror and tell yourself that you are a miracle from God, made by God. Nobody has to look too far to see miracles, so just look around. We are all miracles, the true workmanship of God. God's miracles are everywhere, just open your eyes to this truth and your life will never have the same meaning again. Psalm 34:8 states, "Blessed is the man who takes refuge in him". Know this, as you move forward in your relationship with God, Jesus Christ and the Holy Spirit, you are never alone, and have never been alone, but now in Christ you know it. Once I came to this place of assurance, I realized I don't have to concern myself with anything except belief and faith in my Lord and Savior, Jesus Christ, and be obedient and steadfast to His truth and keep my eyes on Him at all times. Jesus Christ is my anchor.

My brothers and sisters, you are not alone; you've never been alone. Come to the Father through Jesus Christ and have a relationship with Him. As we pray in the name of Jesus Christ, through the authority of Jesus Christ, it means that He is our mediator. Jesus Christ has authorized us to pray with His authority to our Father in heaven. Remember that Jesus is the ultimate authority. This is a precious truth in the life of the believer in Christ Jesus. Prayer is vital and a true gift as we walk in our truth in Jesus Christ, so pray to God and truly be thankful that your life is special to God in heaven through Jesus Christ.

CHAPTER 7

The Power of the Holy Spirit (Resurrection Power)

1 John 4:13 states, "By this we know that we abide in him and he in us, because he has given us of his Spirit." When we believe in Christ as our Lord and Savior, we are immediately given the gift of the Holy Spirit. We are in Christ and Christ is in us and the Holy Spirit is our guarantee.

Romans 8:26-30 states, "Likewise the Spirit helps us in our weakness. For we do not know what to pray for as we ought, but the Spirit himself intercedes for us with groanings too deep for words. And he who searches hearts knows what is the mind of the Spirit, because the Holy Spirit intercedes for the saints according to the will of God. And we know that for those who love God all things work together for good, for those who are called according to his purpose. For those whom he foreknew he also predestined to be conformed to the image of his Son, in order that he might be the firstborn among many brothers.

And those whom he predestined he also called, and those whom he called he also justified, and those whom he justified he also glorified."

These scriptures are so impactful for me as a believer in Jesus Christ, for so many reasons. First off, these verses reaffirm within my spirit that God foreknew me; before I was even alive. God knew before my life even existed that I was predestined to be in Christ and be "like" Christ, and a new creature in Christ. God has "called" all of us into Christ, into His glory and purpose. In Christ, those of us who believe are living for God's glory, and not for our own. This is our truth in Christ.

These verses also share with me that I am never alone in this world as I have been given His Spirit, the Holy Spirit, to be with me at all times, interceding for me in prayer and giving me a spirit of discernment to navigate through every moment of my life. God has also given me His resurrection power, through the Holy Spirit, for God's glory and His true purpose for me. God's resurrection power is unlimited, and all who believe dwell in this same resurrection power through the Holy Spirit, and this power dwells in us. Need I say more?

This is an incredible gift from God. We have the Holy Spirit dwelling in us as an encourager, once we believe and have faith in Christ as our Lord and Savior. We are being transformed and molded into the image of Christ Jesus by the Holy Spirit every single moment. As I look back at my life, and take a real introspective look at the different directions in which I was going as a young person and as an adult, I realize that even before I had received Jesus Christ as my Lord and Savior, I was being guided for God's purpose since I had been predestined to be in Christ already. Once I had believed in Jesus Christ and was blessed with the Holy Spirit, my life changed forever. In fact, I became a new creation in Jesus Christ.

Now I am living in Christ, and Christ lives through me, with an incredible power and force. This truth is real, exciting, and obvious as I can clearly see how the Spirit affects my life day by day. I can truly feel the Holy Spirit in me, particularly when I am going down a path that is not in my purpose in Christ. I can feel an unsettling feeling inside my spirit when I, sometimes, do things on my own and in my flesh, and not in the Spirit of Christ, which is in me. This is important as we move forward in walking and dwelling in our purpose in Christ. We should trust God and Jesus Christ in every way, and learn to listen to the Holy Spirit who is guiding us in our purpose in Christ. We are alive because of God's grace and purpose for us for His glory.

Ephesians 1:13-14 states, "In him you also, when you heard the word of truth, the gospel of your salvation, and believed in him, were sealed with the promised Holy Spirit, who is the guarantee of our inheritance until we acquire possession of it, to the praise of his glory." This verse talks about the significant truth that the Holy Spirit "seals us." To me this means that the Holy Spirit won't allow anything to penetrate my salvation in Christ and my relationship with God. We are sealed with the promised Holy Spirit which is our "guarantee" of our inheritance in Christ, until we acquire possession of it. This is our promise from God through the Holy Spirit, and the grace that our Father has given to us through faith, in Jesus Christ. It's a promise and God never breaks a promise. Take this truth into your heart right now, and know that you are sealed in Christ for eternity. 2 Corinthians 5:5 states, "He who has prepared us for this very thing is God, who has given us the Spirit as a guarantee." The Holy Spirit is our guarantee that we are in Christ forever. We who believe are now sealed by the Holy Spirit in Jesus Christ.

Ephesians 3:16-20 states, "That according to the riches of his glory he may grant you to be strengthened with power through his Spirit in your inner being, so that Christ may dwell in your hearts through faith – that you, being rooted and grounded in love, may have strength to comprehend with all the saints what is the breadth and length and height and depth, and to know the love of Christ that surpasses knowledge, that you may be filled with all the fullness of God. Now to him who is able to do far more abundantly than all that we ask or think, according to the power at work within us, to him be glory in the church and in Christ Jesus throughout all generations, forever and ever. Amen."

For me, the truth of this particular scripture really brings home the fact that we are not going to, or even have to, understand everything on our own. The Holy Spirit will keep us rooted, entrenched, and grounded in love, as we move forward in our walk in Christ. We are strengthened with resurrection power into our inner most being and spirit, so that Jesus Christ may dwell in our hearts through faith. We will start to comprehend with our brothers and sisters the scope, and height, and depth, just to know that the love of Christ surpasses or exceeds all human knowledge, and that we are filled with the fullness of God. We will do far greater things with the Holy Spirit in us, than we could have ever thought possible, to give glory to God. Jesus tells us in Mark 9:23, "If you can! All things are possible for one who believes."

2 Corinthians 3:4-6 states, "Such is the confidence that we have through Christ toward God. Not that we are sufficient in ourselves to claim anything as coming from us, but our sufficiency is from God, who has made us competent to be ministers of a new covenant, not of the letter but of the Spirit." What really touches my heart regarding this truth is that we can have confidence through Jesus Christ towards our Almighty God. Wow, this has changed my life, especially my prayer life and the elements of my life that includes the purpose and trust created by God to this point. The turning point for me is what is being

shaped through fruits and gifts in my life in Christ, which I know has nothing to do with me, but everything to do with God, Christ in my life, and the Holy Spirit dwelling in me. The encouragement, strength, and guidance to manifest glory to God in my life, through the Holy Spirit, are truly a blessing for me. This book is a direct reflection of the Holy Spirit in me through Jesus Christ. It is through the grace of God that I am able to communicate, in a way that is in the Spirit, through the Word of God to all of you who are reading these pages.

I am not sufficient or adequate in myself, but by being in Christ and Christ being in me, I am a conqueror, and I am strengthened daily by the Holy Spirit, for Gods purpose in my life. This book is a direct reflection of Christ in me, and my testimony and God's purpose for me towards His glory, and I believe it is part of my truth in Christ Jesus and what manifests from it.

Galatians 5:22-25 states, "But the fruit of the Spirit is love, joy, peace, patience, kindness, goodness, faithfulness, gentleness, self-control; against such things there is no law. And those who belong to Christ Jesus have crucified the flesh with its passions and desires. If we live by the Spirit, let us also walk by the Spirit." Our fruits or gifts come from God and the Holy Spirit, through Christ, and from these types of fruits there is no law or commandment. In my life the spirit of love commands my every action to all that I contact on a daily basis. This is not an earthly love that we sometimes feel, but a spiritual love that transcends everything in this world. God's love is so gentle and for-giving in every way, and this love is deep in my spirit, especially when it comes to people that are struggling or unable to protect themselves. I love people with all my heart and I know this strong and deep love comes from God through the Holy Spirit, not from my 'old self.'

Romans 5:5 states, "And hope does not put us to shame, because God's love has been poured into our hearts through the Holy Spirit who has been given to us." God's love has been poured inside my heart through the Holy Spirit, and it is this truth of scripture that tells me that God loves me in every way as His adopted son in Christ. Not only did He give up His Son Jesus Christ for me and my sins through grace, but God has given me His love through the Holy Spirit. Think about it for a second- *God's love has been poured into those who believe in Christ through the Holy Spirit through faith.* God is love and if He has been poured in us, through Jesus Christ, then God's love is in us through Jesus Christ. What a true gift and blessing. Think about the impact you can make on people's lives with God's love running through you towards others.

1 Corinthians 3:16 states, "Do you not know that you are God's temple and that God's Spirit dwells in you?" To know that God's Holy Spirit dwells in me is a truth that strikes me every day when I wake up. I was created to be a temple, as a Holy place for God's Spirit. The Holy Spirit is dwelling in me right now, and the truth that I am in Christ and Christ is in me, is the most incredible truth to ever make sense. *It's the only truth that does make sense to me about life.* Through faith in Jesus Christ, He gives us His Spirit and we are one with His Spirit through faith. In Luke 12:8-12 Jesus says, "And I tell you, everyone who acknowledges me before men, the Son of Man also will acknowledge before the angels of God, but the one who denies me before men will be denied before the angels of God. And everyone who speaks a word against the Son of Man will be forgiven, but the one who blasphemes against the Holy Spirit will not be forgiven. And when they bring you before the synagogues and the rulers and the authorities, do not be anxious about how you should defend yourself or what you should say, for the Holy Spirit will teach you in that very hour what you ought to say."

The Holy Spirit, through faith, will teach or show us how and what to speak when we can't speak for ourselves. God teaches us everything through the Holy Spirit, so we don't need to be anxious about anything. The Word of God also teaches us to never blaspheme, disrespect, or curse the Holy Spirit. I'm so thankful that the Holy Spirit is with me in my life, because I know I am never alone, even at the lowest of moments of my life. I am protected by God, and as a believer I am one in Christ with the Holy Spirit, for all times. If you are in Christ, which I pray you are, you are also one in Christ with the Holy Spirit for all times. 1 Corinthians 6:19-20 states, "Or do you not know that your body is a temple of the Holy Spirit within you, whom you have from God? You are not your own for you were bought with a price."

Romans 8:16-17 states, "The Spirit himself bears with our spirit that we are children of God, and if children, then heirs—heirs of God and fellow heirs with Christ, provided we suffer with him in order that we may also be glorified with him." 1 John 5:6 states, "This is he who came by water and blood – Jesus Christ; not by the water only but by the water and the blood. And the Spirit is the one who testifies, because the Spirit is the truth. For there are three that testify, the Spirit and the water and the blood and these three agree." Let us talk about truth and what it means in our lives. To me the truth of scripture is the ultimate standard and the foundation of my life in Christ Jesus. I am in faith, as this truth of scripture is a certainty to me even though I fall short in my daily walk, but I know that my Lord Jesus Christ of Nazareth never fell short in His walk, which is why this covenant was made by God with Jesus Christ. I am in Christ and that is why I am righteous and justified in God's eyes.

We think we can go through life and nobody will know what we think or do, but the Spirit is truth. The Holy Spirit testifies to our heart and spirit about what is right with our Father in heaven, and our Lord and Savior Jesus Christ. Sometimes we just get the feeling that we are not in a good place, or we know we are doing something wrong and that unsettling feeling talks to us. That feeling that affects my spirit is the Holy Spirit, working through my spirit, to bring my true path in Christ into my life here in this world. The Holy Spirit is also my guide towards my truth in Christ Jesus.

I pray that the Holy Spirit guides you in your prayers and your lives, all the time knowing that the Holy Spirit and the love of God is dwelling in you. Maturing us so we are more in line with the Holy Spirit inside us, so the Spirit can guide us to the path that God wants us to be on, and for which we are being equipped through Jesus Christ. The Holy Spirit bears with our spirit that we are children of God, and if children, then heirs, and fellow heirs with Christ. This is the most magnificent and amazing gift of grace from God that I can grasp in my life. In Christ we are truly a child of God and the Holy Spirit himself bears witness to this fact in our spirit. When moving through your path and through truth in Christ, remember this fact- if a believer is in Christ through Christ, they are a child of the most high God through Christ, and the Holy Spirit bears witness to this truth. The Holy Spirit is our witness and our guarantee. Every blessing we have ever needed in our life is available for us right now through faith. Take ownership of it and thank Jesus Christ for it.

1 Corinthians 12:3-11 states, "Therefore I want you to understand that no one speaking in the Spirit of God ever says "Jesus is accursed!" And no one can say "Jesus is Lord" except in the Holy Spirit. Now there are varieties of gifts, but the same Spirit, and there are varieties of service, but the same Lord; and there are varieties of activities, but it is the same God who empowers them all in everyone. To each is

given the manifestation of the Spirit for the common good. For to one is given through the Spirit the utterance of wisdom, and to another the utterance of knowledge according to the same Spirit, to another faith by the same Spirit, to another gifts of healing by the one Spirit, to another prophecy, to another the ability to distinguish between spirits, to another various kinds of tongues, to another the interpretation of tongues. All these are empowered by one and the same Spirit, who apportions to each one individually as he wills." In thinking and praying about the purpose or will of God in our lives, let us remember that we all have different gifts and talents given to us by God, but we all have the same Lord in Jesus Christ, and it is our God who empowers all of us through Jesus Christ and the Holy Spirit. This is the truth of life in Christ that God gives us all power and life, and always has, and always will. There are a variety of gifts and a variety of services that God has willed for all those who believe.

This truth is a blessing in every way because for me it means that I only have to recognize the gifts that God has predestined for me, and recognize what is in my spirit to stay in faith regarding my truth and purpose. God has already apportioned or divided and allocated His fruits and gifts between all who believe, depending on His purpose for us for His glory. It has already been established and it is already done. *We don't have to go looking for it, as it is already in us.* This is fundamental and key to what the Holy Spirit is moving through me in this book and in my life. I now know that I have already been established in His love, purpose, and truth in Christ. I have been given resurrection power, through the Holy Spirit in Christ, to establish and dwell in this truth as a new creature in Christ, rooted in grace. Jesus Christ is our truth, and in Christ He will come out of us for His glory for God's purpose.

Philippians 2:1-2 states, "So if there is any encouragement in Christ, any comfort from love, and participation in the Spirit, any affection and sympathy, complete my joy by being of the same mind, having the same love, being in full accord and of one mind." This scripture touches my spirit in so many ways. It states that we are to be fully encouraged and to have complete confidence and hope in Christ. We should always be comforted and relaxed, with no anxieties, as we dwell in Christ's eternal and unlimited love, and to have faith and fully take part with the Holy Spirit. To have a place or purpose in Christ, by being of the same mind as Christ, and dwelling in the same love as Christ, being in one accord with Christ, is the truest blessing of dwelling in our truth in Christ. In His love and peace in the Spirit is the ultimate gift of being in Christ.

Titus 3:5-7 states, "He saved us, not because of works done by us in righteousness, but according to his own mercy, by the washing of regeneration and renewal of the Holy Spirit, whom he poured out on us richly through Jesus Christ our Savior, so that being justified by his grace we might become heirs according to the hope of eternal life." We should always remember this reality, moving forward in our truth in Christ, that Christ saved us not because of work done by ourselves, but according to His own mercy, by the washing or regeneration of our spirits. No longer being rooted in Adam, and the sinful nature that was to follow, but now being rooted in grace through the renewal of being born again in Jesus Christ, and the gift of the Holy Spirit, whom God poured on you and me in Christ. God actually regenerated, or essentially, in its purest sense, *formed us again and renewed our spirits.* God has justified us through His grace, that we might become heirs in Christ. Our spirits are completely justified and sanctified, once and for all, in our Lord and Savior Jesus Christ. Hebrews 10:10 states, "And by that will we have been sanctified through the offering of the body of Jesus Christ once for all." It's done in Jesus Christ. We have inherited as a new creation in Christ what God wanted us to have through Christ, according to the hope of eternal everlasting life in Christ.

This is my ultimate truth in Christ. *I have inherited or been given eternal life in Christ Jesus with God and the Holy Spirit. There is nothing that is or could be greater for me in my life, and in fact, life finally makes sense. It's absolutely incredible how God works. Praise you Jesus.*

CHAPTER 8

God in Our Life through the Gospel (The Ultimate Standard of Truth)

I truly believe, in my spirit, that to have an intimate and trusting relationship with God, Jesus Christ, and the Holy Spirit, we must spend quality time in His Word every day. It's also important to spend our time in consistent prayer on a daily basis, so we can become closer to our Father in heaven, as we get to know the truth about our salvation in Christ Jesus through the Word of God.

My life started having more clarity and blessings in my daily walk and purpose in Christ when I truly let go and made a daily commitment to spend quality time dwelling in and praying on the Word of God, and building my relationship with Jesus Christ. Morning and evening and throughout the day I spend time in the Word of God, and it nourishes me with discernment about His truth and about my Lord and Savior, God and the Holy Spirit. 2 Timothy 3:16 states, "All scripture is breathed out by God and profitable for teaching, for reproof, for correction, and for training in righteousness, that the man of God may be competent, equipped for every good work." This is a critical verse as it means that all scripture "was breathed out by God," for the believer's edification, and that the scripture is alive. 2 Peter 1:21 states, "For no prophecy was ever produced by the will of man, but men spoke from God as they were carried along by the Holy Spirit." To me this standard of truth states that man did not make up what was written in the Bible, but was inspired by the Holy Spirit for every Word that was written in the Word of God. The same Holy Spirit that dwells in the believer right now carried the men along that spoke the Word from God.

The men who wrote these words were inspired by the Holy Spirit with every word that has been written and documented in the Holy Bible. The Word of God is the very breath of life to me, in every way, while I'm on this Earth. I can turn to the Word of God and learn everything that God wants me to know regarding His truth and how it relates to my life in Christ at any time. In my life, I am clinging to the Holy Word of God in its truth and strength for my life. The Word of God brings His children closer to Him and Jesus Christ, and is the ultimate gift from our Father in heaven. The Holy Spirit gives us encouragement and guidance in our daily lives so that we can walk in His truth and purpose for His glory. The true gift of meditating in His Word and prayer is having more of God and Jesus Christ in our lives, and the strength of the Holy Spirit running through us. The Holy Spirit gives us strength, peace, and discernment, as He guides us forward into God's purpose for us. Our truth in Christ is Christ in all the aspects of our lives. Christ through us.

Romans 1:16-17 states, "For I am not ashamed of the gospel, for it is the power of God for salvation to everyone who believes, to the Jew first and also to the Greek. For in it the righteousness of God is revealed from faith for faith, as it is written, "the righteousness shall live by faith." This tells me that I should never be ashamed at all about the Word of God, and that it should be a cornerstone of my life's foundational truth. The Word of God is the power of God moving through us who believe through faith as we abide in Jesus Christ. In the Bible, the righteousness of God is exposed to all who believe in faith. The Holy Bible is a mirror into our truth in Jesus Christ and it shows us our identity.

Let me tell you all an intimate story about how much the Word of God means to me. I have gone through very trying and tough times in my life, as we all have, but I have found ultimate peace in having the Word of God right next to me most of the time. This includes not only reading and praying on the truth of the Holy Bible and the truth and enlightenment that is given to me by God Himself through the scripture, but also keeping the Holy Bible next to me whether I'm in a meeting, in my car, or sleeping. That's right, there have been times in my life when I have been in strong prayer about an anxiety or fear that I am battling, and I have held onto my Bible at all times. This may sound a bit unusual, but I find solace in embracing my Holy Bible. I can only say this- it's peaceful for me to know that not only is the Word of God in my Spirit through spending time in scripture, but also to have the Good Book right next to me when I sleep at times. The Word of God is alive. It's a constant reminder for me of my truth in Christ Jesus as my Lord and Savior. Give it a try and spend quality time with your Bible right now, and don't let go.

I notice that spiritual attacks not only come in the days, but a majority of the times for me, I have seen attacks come in the middle of the night, and having my Bible close to me brings me a certain type of peace, knowing that the Word of God is right next to me and in me. I can't explain it, but I am reminded of my peace when the Holy Bible is right next to me, along with the critical importance of spending time in it. What a gift from God. The Word of God is alive as God is speaking to us through His Word. I want to be in His Word as much as possible in my daily life, and I know it brings me closer to God and the truth He wants for my life for His glory.

Matthew 24:35 states, "Heaven and earth will pass away, but my words will not pass away." The words of truth in the Word of God will never die and will never pass away. They are everlasting and eternal, and they will never cease from being breathed out by God through the Holy Spirit. Jesus shared in John 17:14-19, "I have given them the word, and the world has hated them because they are not of the world, just as I am not of the world. I do not ask that you take them out of the world, but that you keep them from the evil one. They are not of the world, just as I am not of the world, so I have sent them into the world. And for their sake I consecrate myself, that they also be sanctified in truth." Jesus has asked God to keep us from the evil one in this verse, as we are no longer of this world as believers in Jesus Christ. We are now a part of the kingdom of God, and the Father has sent us into the world to be His children and to be a light for the world, as Christ has been made holy, so that we are now holy in Christ is the ultimate truth of His Word. This is an ultimate gift of truth from our Lord and Savior, that through Him we are righteous and sanctified in Christ for eternity. The veil has been lifted once and for all in Christ.

Psalm 119:89 states, "Forever, O Lord, your word is firmly fixed in the heavens." This verse brings me ultimate peace, in that His Word or His divine utterance is firmly fixed, meaning that it will never cease on Earth or in heaven, and is eternal. O Lord, thank you so much that your Word will live forever. The Word of God is used to teach and is used for a standard of how to live our lives correctly, and in accordance with God, through His Holy Word. The Word of God is truth in regards to how we are to be built up in our lives and trained in God's way for us for His glory.

In my heart I know that the Holy Spirit gives me discernment through God's Word and its ultimate truth. I want to continually grow in prayer so that the Holy Spirit will give me the ability to understand or discern what the scripture is saying to me, for my life in Christ, so I can touch and impact others in Christ. When walking in my truth in Christ I cling to God's Word as it gives me direction, so I can be a blessing for others' lives as well as my own. We can fulfill our purpose if we repeatedly dwell, focus, and trust in the Word of God. God is speaking through the Word of God to His children through Christ and the Holy Spirit. God is guiding us through His truth in the Word of God, and that's why the Bible is so important for the believer. Our truth in Christ has been manifested through the Word of God for the believer's life. Dwell in the Word, my brothers and sisters, and be nourished and walk in your truth in Christ Jesus.

CHAPTER 9

Dwelling in Christ
(From Now to Forever)

Matthew 11:28-30 states, "Come to me, all who labor and are heavy laden, and I will give you rest. Take my yoke upon you, and learn from me, for I am gentle and lowly in heart, and you will find rest for your souls. For my yoke is easy, and my burden is light." Since Christ has been my Lord and Savior, I have become enlightened over time, through the Holy Spirit, that my true peace and rest lies in Jesus alone, not in what I can do for myself, or what this world can do for me. Jesus wants me to love Him with all my heart and as I walk in my truth in Christ, I find it absolutely necessary to continually pray for His strength so I can let go, and take on the yoke of Jesus, and cast all my anxieties and worries at the foot of the cross, and let them go now and forever.

Jesus wants us to trust that He will always take care of us, and in my life He always has, no matter what. Jesus wants us to recognize that He is gentle and loving and has died for us in every way, and His love for us is beyond words. Jesus wants us to learn from Him and take from His Word and pray that our lives will manifest in a way that is like Jesus, especially in how we touch other people's lives. This is an important verse for me as it always brings rest to my spirit when I pray on it. I rely on Jesus to guide me through all the difficulties and challenges that may come my way no matter what. As we walk in Christ we can trust that He is watching over us, and will always be there to love us, strengthen us, and protect us in every part of our lives. So as we walk, let us walk in faith, through the yoke of Jesus Christ, and He will guide our hearts into His peace.

It is written in John 15:1-17 that Jesus tells us, "I am the true vine, and my Father is the vinedresser. Every branch in me that does not bear fruit he takes away, and every branch that does bear fruit he prunes, that it may bear more fruit. Already you are clean because of the word that I have spoken to you. Abide in me, and I in you. As the branch cannot bear fruit by itself, unless it abides in the vine, neither can you, unless you abide in me. I am the vine; you are the branches. Whoever abides in me and I in him, he it is that bears much fruit, for apart from me you can do nothing. If anyone does not abide in me he is thrown away like a branch and withers; and the branches are gathered, thrown into the fire, and burned. If you abide in me, and my words abide in you, ask whatever you wish, and it will be done for you. By this my Father is glorified, that you bear much fruit and so prove to be my disciples. As the Father has loved me, so have I loved you. Abide in my love. If you keep my commandments, you will abide in my love, just as I have kept my Father's commandments and abide in his love. These things I have spoken to you, that my joy may be in you, and that your joy may be full. This is my commandment, that you love one another as I have loved you. Greater love has no one than this that someone lay down his life for his friends. You are my friends if you do what I command you. No longer do I call you servants, for the servant does not know what his master is doing; but I have called you friends, for all that I have heard from my Father I have made known to you. You did not choose me, but I chose you and appointed you that you should go and bear fruit and that your fruit should abide, so that whatever you ask the Father in my name, he may give it to you. These things I command you, so that you will love one another."

This scripture always touches me in a strong way in continuing to develop the theme of what I am sharing with you in regards to walking in our truth in Christ. Jesus states to "abide in Me, and I in you." To me this means that we are dwelling in each other and we are now one. We are together and nothing can break us apart. *Christ my Lord and Savior in me, and I in Him.* Take some time to think about this. When we walk in Christ, we are walking as one through faith in Him. I want to remind everyone that this incredible truth comes through God's grace and nothing else, especially our own doing. It's God's mercy, love, and the blood of the Lamb, which is Jesus Christ, our Lord that has made all this happen through grace as His blood now covers us. We do nothing to deserve this truth, so I pray that you will rest in this truth, and the grace of God, and dwell in Him. It's already been done for us in Christ. It's completely unmerited favor for the believer.

Christ is the vine, and God is the vinedresser, and we who believe in faith are the branches and we can't do anything apart from God, which means that God is in control of everything. God has given us freedom to choose in our lives, but He is sovereign in all of our choices. I believe that God works in all of our choices, either good or bad, and will always show us His way if we are looking towards Him for His glory. If someone is not in the vine they will be thrown away and will wither or basically fade away. *I believe the true meaning and purpose for life is to accept and receive God's free gift of grace, and accept Jesus Christ as your Lord and Savior.*

The challenge is to let go of our old self and trust in Him for everything. His joy and love is in us, and that's what makes our joy and love complete, because Christ can now be our source for life. Knowing that Jesus laid down His life for me brings me to my knees in overwhelming gratitude, and awakens my spirit to share with others what Jesus has done for me. This is a major reason why I decided to write this book, so I would have the opportunity to share what Christ has done for me in my life. Christ is my Lord and Savior, and now my friend, and I now look to Him for everything in my life.

Now I realize that He has already given me everything I need. I only need to receive it. I know in my spirit that Christ is guiding me in every way and protecting me, and has a plan for me, but I must walk by faith, and in faith, and move forward through the life that He has given to me. To know that He chose me before time even existed, and appointed or selected me to be in His family, brings me to my knees in thankfulness. I thank you Father God, my Lord and Savior Jesus Christ, and the Holy Spirit for my new life in Christ.

Through faith and belief, we know that God blesses us when we accept Christ into our hearts. At that point, we our dwelling in Christ and He in us, and Jesus will never let us go. I have this overwhelming feeling of peace, joy and thankfulness that flows through me when I take the time to truly wrap myself around this truth. Christ says to go out and love one another as He has loved us. So a big part of walking in our truth in Christ is to love each other unconditionally, and He will give us the ability to always reconcile ourselves to others if that needs to be done. Walk in your truth in Christ, and abide in the vine by walking in His love and sharing God's love with others. Share the incredible news of grace with people that touch your life.

1 Thessalonians 5:23 states, "Now may the God of peace himself sanctify you completely, and may your whole spirit and soul and body be kept blameless at the coming of our Lord Jesus Christ." If you really think about it, this is the best news of all. *We are being transformed by the Holy Spirit in Christ, through our faith that God has blessed us with, and our spirit is sanctified once and for all in Christ.* This is the peace and hope that believers speak of when sharing the good news with others that they can dwell in Christ's peace and righteousness in Christ, through faith and belief in Jesus Christ as our Lord and Savior. Think about this truth, that the God of Peace Himself, the Creator of the universe and everything in it, has sanctified our spirits when we receive Christ, and through the Holy Spirit is transforming our soul, mind, and body into becoming more like Christ.

Romans 8:11-17 states, "If the Spirit of him who raised Jesus from the dead dwells in you, he who raised Christ Jesus from the dead will give life to your mortal bodies through his Spirit who dwells in you. So then, brothers, we are debtors, not to the flesh, to live according to the flesh. For if you live according to the flesh you will die, but if by the Spirit you put to death the deeds of the body, you will live. For all who are led by the Spirit of God are sons of God. For you did not receive the spirit of slavery to fall back into fear, but you have received the Spirit of adoption as sons, by whom we cry, "Abba! Father!" The Spirit himself bears witness with our spirit that we are children of God, and if children, then heirs—heirs of God and fellow heirs with Christ, provided we suffer with him in order that we may also be glorified with him."

To be an heir or a beneficiary of God through Jesus Christ is to say that all that is Christ's is ours, as long as we are in Christ. Christ's love, His peace, His joy, His patience, His kindness, His suffering, His goodness, His faithfulness, His gentleness, and His self-control and all that is Christ, is now ours in Christ. As a new creation in Christ when we love someone it will be the type of love that Christ is. In Christ we now share His love with others as He lives in us through the Holy Spirit. It is no longer our old love that we will be sharing and manifesting in our lives, but Christ's love coming through us that will be stirring and impacting other people's lives as we now radiate Jesus out of us. We love because God has loved us through Christ, and He is giving us Christ's love in our hearts towards all people. When God gives us Christ's peace as an heir in Christ, He is giving us the belief and tranquility that is only in Christ.

True peace is what people are always searching for. To truly find peace is to be in Christ and to dwell in His peace, and also be able to experience the unstoppable joy of Jesus Christ while dwelling in His joy, and His joy in us is a true gift in every way. To be truly joyful in Christ's joy, and be delighting in the blessings of this life as we experience our lives, is impossible on our own or through worldly desires, but only through faith in Christ Jesus, can that joy be experienced and released through Him in any situation of our lives.

Patience is a quality that believers can only experience through Christ, especially when the world can sway us and push us like the ocean pushes the water. For me, patience and peace go hand in hand, so I must cling to my faith as I am being pushed in so many directions, by so many people, emotions, and thoughts in this world. To walk in my truth in Christ, I will need Christ's patience, not my old self's level of patience. The strength and endurance that I have received in Christ is moving me into my true purpose for His glory. But as you move into your truth in Christ, you can now have the patience level of Christ in your walk and life, and you will feel a serenity that I know can only be felt in Christ. You will not become discouraged, but you will be encouraged through Christ's patience in you. This is truly a gift of the spirit.

Let's talk about the kindness of Jesus and how this quality or fruit is now part of a believer in Christ. Jesus felt an overwhelming compassion for those in need, especially the sinner and the people who were lost and sick. Jesus knew that His ministry was to save the sinners. We were all born into sin nature on this Earth, but Jesus was willing to be put to death on a cross to save the believer, through faith, because of His compassion and His love for those who believe. His kindness was evident in His ministry and His walk in all the blessings He gave freely to those in need. All who believed in Him were touched by His kindness and blessed in every way. His kindness in me has changed my life in every way, in every moment of my life, as a child of God through Christ. I can't help but be loving, sympathetic, compassionate, gentle, kindhearted, and thoughtful towards others around me.

Again, it is not me, but Christ coming through me. Jesus is where these fruits of the Spirit come. As a new believer, our old self is dead, and our new nature in Christ Jesus is alive and born again, and you will notice a shift, or change in how you think, feel, and act towards others. This is the process of letting go of your older self, although your spirit is completely righteous, you will continue to grow in Christ as the Holy Spirit encourages you, and the Word of God clings to you. I pray that you take on the yoke or Spirit of Christ in your life. Dwell and abide in Christ in your life, and walk in your truth in Christ.

Christ's goodness, His gentleness, and His self control will also be a part of our lives now in Christ, especially when it comes to others around us, particularly those who are hurting and in need, and those who are lonely and scared. We should constantly pray for those gifts of Christ's Spirit to continue to expand in our lives through the Holy Spirit, so we can be the light on Earth in Christ. We are now the calm and gentleness for people as Christ's Ambassadors, as we constantly shine Christ's goodness and love on and towards others. As a believer you will still fall short, but you will not be a slave to sin anymore if you truly are in Christ. You will have a discernment or knowledge of your sin, and the Holy Spirit will convict you inside your heart when you do fall short, and you will know that is not Christ's path for you. You will make a choice to cease being a slave to all sin, and acknowledge and repent your sin to God when you do sin. You now have the self-control in Christ in every way, so pray for Christ's strength and walk in authority in your life, and watch how your life will increase in Christ for His glory. Look around you right now and see where you can make a positive impact in a gentle, loving way, and fight for the good. You now have the goodness and gentleness of Christ in you. Use it.

Galatians 2:20 states, "I have been crucified with Christ. It is no longer I who live, but Christ who lives in me. The life I now live in the flesh, I live by faith in the Son of God, who loved me and gave himself for me." God gives the believer the ability and strength to walk in faith; it is not from our old sinful self. We have the gift of faith in Christ, through Jesus Christ, to dwell in Christ. It has nothing to do with us at all, but it's God's grace that shines on us as He has chosen us for adoption through Jesus. If you are now in Christ, He chose you my brother and sister.

Romans 6:5-11 states, "For if we have been united with him in a death like his, we shall certainly be united with him in a resurrection like his. We know that our old self was crucified with him in order that the body of sin might be brought to nothing, so that we would no longer be enslaved to sin. For one who has died has been set free from sin. Now if we have died with Christ, we believe that we will also live with him. We know that Christ, being raised from the dead, will never die again; death no longer has dominion over him. For the death he died he died to sin, once for all, but the life he lives he lives to God. So you also must consider yourselves dead to sin and alive to God in Christ Jesus."

In Christ we have been united with Him in His death, and we shall be united with Him in His resurrection. Our old self is crucified with Him, so that what was our sin may be brought to nothing, so that we will no longer be a slave to sin ever again in Christ. Once we have died from sin through Christ, we are free from sin for eternity through grace. Believers know that they will dwell in Christ forever, as we who believe know that Jesus was raised from the dead and will never die again, as Christ defeated death once and for all. Christ lived for God, and we shall live for Christ and God and the Holy Spirit. We walk in this truth that we are now 'dead to sin and alive to God in Christ Jesus' and live our lives for God. I would say this about my truth in Christ- my life is not about me anymore; it is about Christ and God in my life, and what my purpose is for the Kingdom of Heaven. *Living Christ through me is now my life purpose in Christ.*

2 Corinthians 1:21-22 states, "And it is God who establishes us with you in Christ, and has anointed us, and who has also put his seal on us and given us his Spirit in our hearts as a guarantee." What is our guarantee so that we know that we know? Our guarantee is that we are established and recognized by God the creator through Jesus Christ. God has anointed us and has put His seal on those who believe in Jesus Christ as their Lord and Savior. God has given us who believe His Spirit in our heart, as a guarantee that we are in Christ eternally. We have been purchased, and we are Christ's, and He will never let us go. Remember that when you feel alone and you become unsure. We are still human and made of flesh, but we walk in His spirit as we are being

transformed. God is perfect. We are now in Christ through faith, and Christ is our savior, and our guarantee is the Holy Spirit in us. Don't ever let go of this truth.

Philippians 3:8-11 states, "Indeed, I count everything as loss because of the surpassing worth of knowing Christ Jesus my Lord. For his sake I have suffered the loss of all things and count them as rubbish, in order that I may gain Christ and be found in him, not having a righteousness of my own that comes from the law, but that which comes through faith in Christ, the righteousness from God that depends on faith – that I may know him and the power of his resurrection, and may share his sufferings, becoming like him in his death, that by any means possible I may attain the resurrection from the dead." 1 John 2: 27-28 states, "But the anointing that you received from him abides in you, and you have no need that anyone should teach you. But as his anointing teaches you about everything, and is true, and is no lie—just as it has taught you, abide in him. And now, little children, abide in him, so that when he appears we may have confidence and not shrink from him in shame at his coming." I have put these two scriptures together because it simply tells me that nothing really matters except to be found in Christ, and that my righteousness has everything to do with this fact and truth. I can do nothing, and I have done nothing, and I have nothing at all to do except abide in Jesus Christ. It is not about the law, but about faith in Jesus Christ. I now know Him and the power of His resurrection, as I am now in the resurrection as well. I am dead to sin.

Now my life is focused on my walk in my truth in Christ, which will not have anything to do with me, but everything to do with the anointing and blessing that I receive in Christ and from the Word of God. The Holy Spirit abides in me and He will teach and anoint me with all truth regarding everything I need for my life. There is only truth in

God's Word, and there is absolutely no lying or falseness in His Word. Christ is Truth. We now abide or dwell in Jesus Christ, so that when He appears in our lives we will have the confidence to not shrink from Him in shame. Walking in faith in Christ will show us our purpose in Christ.

In John 17:19-24 Jesus tells His Father, "And for their sake I consecrate myself, that they also may be sanctified in truth. I do not ask for these only, but also for those who will believe in me through their word, that they may all be one, just as you, father, are in me, and I in you, that they also may be in us, so that the world may believe that you have sent me. The glory that you have given me I have given to them, that they may be one even as we are one, I in them and you in me, that they may become perfectly one, so that the world may know that you sent me and loved them even as you loved me. Father, I desire that they also, whom you have given me, may be with me where I am, to see my glory that you have given me because you loved me before the foundation of the world." Let's dwell in Christ through the scripture by understanding and coming to the realization that Christ, the Father, and the Holy Spirit are one. That our spirits are now sanctified in this truth, and all truth regarding God's purpose and His Word shows us that we are not only in Christ, but we are in God through Christ as Christ is in God and His Spirit dwells in us. Christ has done this so that, we as believers can be one family, perfectly one in Christ, and that we can know that God loves us as God loves Jesus. In Christ we dwell in the Father, the Son, and the Holy Spirit, and they dwell in us as believers in Christ.

Children of God, through Jesus Christ, I pray you see this truth that God has given through Jesus Christ before the foundation of the world. As I write about these truths, I am completely enlightened, fulfilled, and thankful that I am one in Christ, and my Father in heaven as the Holy Spirit dwells in me. This gives me the strength to move forward in my life and in my truth in Christ, as I know it's not about me. I am no longer walking alone but I am together with God, Jesus Christ, and the Holy Spirit as they give me strength through Jesus in my life to walk in His truth. I pray that this truth gives you strength to move forward and walk in your life and truth in Christ, regardless of how life will come at you. But remember, you are not alone as a believer in Christ; you are always with God, Jesus, and the Holy Spirit. "Matthew 28:20, "And behold, I am with you always, to the end of the age."

CHAPTER 10

Mirror Christ and the Word of God (Fruit on the Vine)

A s I dwell in my truth in Jesus Christ, and all the blessings of our Father, I know in my heart through grace and faith, that our Creator looks at me the same exact way He looks at His own Son Jesus. This truth and reality in Christ brings me to a place of joy, peace, and thanksgiving. In this assurance with God, I am mirroring Christ more and more in my daily life. Through prayer, dwelling in the Word of God, and strength from the Holy Spirit, I am maturing in Christ more and more every day. I am representing more characteristics of Jesus Christ with an image of Christ that is radiating out of me. The more I dwell in His truth, the more His character shines through me, and then shines out towards others. Let me reiterate that we do not, or will not, have the ability or understanding on our own to try and do something like mirroring Christ. Through grace, and the Holy Spirit, while dwelling in the Word of God, and being born into a new life in Christ, we can, and will start to mirror Christ and His characteristics in our daily lives by receiving the blessings of Christ that have already been given to us in Christ. Praise Him. The Holy Spirit will give us His discernment and understanding for the Word of God to work in our daily lives so we can start to mirror Jesus Christ and the Word of God.

I would like to discuss some attributes of our Lord and Savior Jesus Christ that we can all pray for, to manifest them into our lives as we walk and shine like Christ. Let's dwell in the fruits of the Spirit, or characteristics of our Lord and Savior Jesus Christ, and get an understanding of how God will manifest these fruits into our lives.

Galatians 5:22-23 states, "But the fruit of the Spirit is love, joy, peace, patience, kindness, goodness, faithfulness, gentleness, self-control, against such things there is no law." The first and most important characteristic of our Lord and Savior is love, and just how important it really is. 1 Corinthians 13:8-13 says it like this, "Love never ends; as for prophecies, they will pass away; as for tongues, they will cease; as for knowledge, it will pass away. For our knowledge is imperfect and our prophecy is imperfect; but when the perfect comes, the imperfect will pass away. When I was a child, I spoke like a child, I thought like a child, I reasoned like a child; when I became a man, I gave up childish ways. For now we see in a mirror dimly, but then face to face. Now I know in part; then I shall understand fully, even as I have been fully understood. So faith, hope, love abide, these three, but the greatest of these is love." Paul is very clear that love will never end as opposed to prophecies, tongues, and knowledge. They will all pass away except for love. For knowledge is imperfect and prophecy is imperfect, but when the perfect comes (Jesus) the imperfect will pass away. Faith, hope, and love abide together, but the greatest of these is love. Love is the greatest gift that God has given to us through Jesus Christ our Lord and Savior. God is love.

Ephesians 5:1-2 says it clearly, "Therefore be imitators of God, as beloved children. And walk in love, as Christ loved us and gave himself up for us, a fragrant offering and sacrifice to God." For those of you who have moved forward in this book, as a born again Christian through faith in Jesus Christ, and through the Holy Spirit, you are now blessed with the fruits of the Spirit. As you are walking in your new life in Christ, you will notice that you will be more loving, understanding, and patient towards the people in your life, and even towards the people that you don't know because God says we are all brothers and sisters. Take some time to reflect on your life, and look to see if and how much more loving you are towards people as you are now in Christ.

If you see that you are not growing in your love for others and counting others more important than yourself, then take some time right now to pray for the strength and ability to let go of your old self, and start to love others unconditionally as Christ loves us. Pray about that moving forward in your life in Christ. Think about how much Jesus loves you, in that He took on your sin and died on a tree for you and me. Love others and pray for the ability to show Christ's love, even when you've never been able to do that in your life up to this point. Now you are a new creature in Christ. In a future chapter called the "Power of Love" we will dig deeper into this fruit of the Spirit. I'm talking about God's love, not man's love.

Let's take a look at the second fruit of the spirit which is 'joy,' which is more than just happiness, but the joy that God gives, as it far exceeds any happiness that you'll ever experience in your life. I'm talking about the fullness of joy that we receive as we get to rejoice in the truth that we are God's children now, in fellowship forever in Christ. To know that He is joyful in us, is something we should be constantly joyous about, plus being joyful over everything about God. Romans 5:2-5 states, "Through him we have also obtained access by faith into this grace in which we stand, and we rejoice in hope of the glory of God. More than that, we rejoice in our sufferings, knowing that suffering produces endurance, and endurance produces character, and character produces hope, and hope does not put us to shame because God's love has been poured into our hearts through the Holy Spirit who has been given to us."

We should be thankful and joyous to the point of screaming and dancing because we now have the right of entry or admittance, by faith, into His grace in which we stand right now, and always will stand, so we rejoice and celebrate in the hope of the glory of God. In Christ, we have the joy inside our spirit of knowing that we are in Christ, justified to God through our faith in our Lord and Savior Jesus Christ. This truth should bring us not only joy, but a peace that no other peace on this Earth can bring. This is the greatest joy in my life, and in fact has made the other joys in my life, like my wife and children, much more joyful within themselves. The Word of God takes it even farther in saying that not only should we rejoice when things are good, but should also rejoice in our sufferings or challenges in life which are difficult. Let's face it, rejoicing or celebrating in the face of challenges or sufferings is downright tough, but Christ can bring hope and peace into all our situations that life can bring. I praise Him for this truth, as I know God has brought me so much peace in my life in the face of challenges. I know it is from God, not from any other place, but from my Father in heaven through my Lord and Savior Jesus Christ through faith. I thank God for every blessing in my life, and I know He will guide me through all the challenges.

Jesus Christ brings us all peace through faith, even when the challenges come into our lives. Our mirroring of Christ will actually produce more hope than we could have ever imagined on our own. Through Christ we will observe a difference or a change in our lives, while we are walking with Christ in our truth in Christ. What a blessing it is that we get to walk with Christ, as He strengthens, nurtures, and raises us up in Him. We will grow in Him and Christ's true character and we will learn to persevere and endure to the end in the hope in Christ. God's perfect love is in you and me right now as we have been blessed with grace and faith in Christ to believe. Let me say this again. God's perfect love and joy is in us right now in Christ. What a blessing. I thank you Jesus for this truth in my life.

Now let's take a look at the next fruit of the spirit as we start to grow and mature in Christ. We will see this fruit called 'peace' more in every aspect of our lives, and our hearts and minds. Romans 5:1 states, "Therefore, since we have been justified by faith, we have peace with God through our Lord Jesus Christ." To me this is the biggest and most important reason to have peace, and that is to know that God is at peace with me, as I was separated from God before Christ. We spoke of this earlier- to be justified in Christ is everything, as now God sees us as He sees His perfect Son Jesus, and that's perfect in every way. Through faith, we are now at peace with God and not in judgment or separated in any way. This is a reason also to rejoice for those who believe in Christ through faith; they now are at peace with God for eternity. Isaiah 26:3 states "You keep him in perfect peace whose mind is stayed on you, because he trusts you."

As I walk in my truth in Christ, I constantly pray for the strength to keep my mind and eyes focused on Jesus and the Word of God at all times. This is the only way to find true peace in the face of any storm. If our mind is on Christ, we will be in perfect peace, but if our mind goes away from Christ it can be a struggle, so keep your lens focused on the Word of God and be in constant prayer at all times. It's important, as we dwell in His peace, that we keep our mind focused on the truths of the Gospel and on our Lord and Savior Jesus Christ. Jesus said in John 16:33, "I have said these things to you, that in me you may have peace. In the world you will have tribulation. But take heart; I have overcome the world." If our hearts and minds are focused on the world and not the Word of God, this world will bring deception and trials. Jesus shared that He has overcome the world forever, and we are now new creations in Christ. The Word of God is how we fight against the deception of this world. Stay focused on the Word of God at all times, and walk in its truth for your life in peace as a believer.

Philippians 4:7 states, "And the peace of God, which surpasses all understanding, will guard your hearts and your minds in Christ Jesus." To know the peace of God and what that actually truly encompasses in our lives is probably something we may not fully know until we get to heaven, but we should always know that God has got our back if we are in Christ. If this is the only thing you keep in your heart, that our creator through Jesus Christ will guard your heart and your minds at all times in Christ Jesus, you will have a higher level of peace. God will never abandon you, nor forsake you at anytime in Christ Jesus. This is true peace to me, knowing that God is always there for me in Christ Jesus, and that I am now His adopted son in Christ Jesus. My mind tries to wrap itself around this fact, but it always fully knocks me off my feet in the enormity of its truth. Dwell in this type of peace and you will walk your true path in Christ with courage. Colossians 3:15 states, "And let the peace of Christ rule in your hearts, to which indeed you were called in one body and be thankful." Yes, be thankful for the peace of Christ that will rule in your heart if you stay focused on Christ and on the truth of the scriptures. We are one in the body of Christ, and with that comes the peace of knowing we are together with Christ, and if one with Christ then we are one with God. This is true and provides everlasting peace.

Now let's talk about a subject that has been a continual work in progress in my transformation. It's called 'patience,' and it is also a fruit of the spirit, and I truly believe that the only reason I have some patience is because of the Holy Spirit working in me. Most people that know me have come to realize that I am generally very reserved and calm, but sometimes I can get emotional, wild, and loud. But mostly I'm very reserved, and could appear very relaxed as I like to observe before I go into a situation. My patience level has grown so much since coming to the Lord and being filled with the Holy Spirit. I see a majority of my growth and how I am professionally due to the patience of Christ in me, but mostly in my personal relationships. I used to just go for it and then ask questions later, but now I take my time when making decisions through prayer, and by communicating with my wife and other trusted people in my life. Patience is praying for discernment from the Lord when making decisions in our lives. It's taking our time for God to show us His way, instead of us holding on or staying in control of our old ways and not trusting our Lord. Patience sometimes shows its face in doing nothing and simply listening instead of talking. This is the type of patience that I want to write to you about because when we are walking in our truth in Christ, then we must definitely pray for this fruit to be apparent in our lives more than ever. Let's see what the Word says about patience.

Paul writes in Ephesians 4:1-3, "I therefore, a prisoner for the Lord, urge you to walk in a manner worthy of the calling to which you have been called, with all humility and gentleness, with patience, bearing with one another in love, eager to maintain the unity of the Spirit in the bond of peace." God wants us to live our lives in a manner that is worthy or equal to the calling to which we have been called as a child of God. God wants us to have humility and gentleness, and to be patient with everyone, and to dwell in His love and be eager or ready to maintain the unity, or oneness of the Spirit in the bond of peace. This bond of peace can't be broken in Christ. This is why patience is such an important step and fruit in the transformation process of our minds. The Holy Spirit will give us the power to not be self serving, but to be patient with our brothers and sisters in Christ.

1 Timothy 1:15-16 states, "The saying is trustworthy and deserving of full acceptance, that Christ Jesus came into the world to save sinners, of whom I am the foremost. But I received mercy for this reason, that in me, as the foremost, Jesus Christ might display his perfect patience as an example to those who were to believe in him for eternal life." Let us think for a minute just how patient God has been towards us, and always is towards His children. The true gift of mercy is that we have the perfect patience in us through Jesus Christ. God sees our perfect patience because Jesus has perfect patience. Wherever you are in your life journey in Christ, just know that God sees you as perfect in Christ, but the Holy Spirit is working in your heart and mind right now, and bringing forth the gift of patience in your lives. If you have been a believer for a while, I would ask you to take a look back to the time when you became a believer and notice just how different and patient you have become since then. Pray for the gift of patience in handling everything in your life, and know when you are being guided by God and when you are trying to control things yourself. This isn't easy, but through prayer those doors will open for you, and some doors may close. Just stay patient and God will show you the path to walk in your truth in Christ and pray that you would walk in God's time, not your time.

Let's talk about the fruits called kindness and goodness. We all know what this means in our lives. Remember the golden rule- treat others as you would want to be treated. I think we should all ask ourselves the question, 'What does kindness and goodness mean to me? How do I show these fruits of the spirit to others?' Proverbs 21:21 states, "Whoever pursues righteousness and kindness will find life, righteousness, and honor." The Word of God says that if you pursue kindness you will find life. This is so important to God because we already know how important love is to God. God is love. Our Lord wants us to be kind and loving to His children.

The fruit of the Spirit I see most in the believer is their kindness and love towards people. Hosea 11: 4 states, "I led them with cords of kindness, with the bands of love, and I became to them as one who eases the yoke on their jaws, and I bent down to them and fed them." In this passage, God is talking about His love for Israel and how God, through His love and kindness, eases the yoke or their burdens and it showed in their faces, and how God fed them. This is a beautiful passage, as it just hits me how God has, and is always being so kind to me, and how He has eased my burdens, and has put the yoke of Christ on me. God is always feeding me His kindness through Christ. I am actually crying right now feeling the effects of Christ in my life, and how I am walking in His truth for me, and feeling the kindness and mercy that God has shown towards me and my family through Jesus Christ. Thank you so much Jesus for my life in you.

In my heart I know that any graciousness that is in me, or that shows itself in my walk, is the goodness from my Lord and Savior Jesus Christ pouring out of me. There was not much good in me before I found Jesus Christ, because it was all about me. Yes, I was generally a nice person, and I tried to be nice to people, but now I display Godly goodness in me since I have Jesus Christ in my life. You cannot have God's goodness in your walk unless you are in Jesus Christ. As you walk in your truth in Christ, your goodness and kindness will be right at the forefront because it will be Christ's goodness and kindness, coming out of you, manifesting in love for others. As you continue to grow in your walk, it will be more about others, and less and less about yourself, and this will be a turning point in your walk in Christ, and a direct reflection of Christ in you. *Live for Christ not for your old self.*

Faithfulness has more to do with God's faithfulness for us through Jesus Christ. Just think about how faithful our Lord has been, and still is to us every second of our lives, and all that He has been faithful towards. Psalm 145:13 says, "The Lord is faithful in all his words and kind in all his works." God's faithfulness shows in all of His words, His kindness, and His works. This means that every single thing that goes on in our lives, bad or good, is ultimately for our good and God's glory in His timing and His plan for us. This is a hard truth to grasp because there are so many tragic events that happen to people on a daily basis and it's hard to understand why. My prayers go out to all the people that are going through times in which they are hurting and people around them are going through pain. I don't understand why things happen, but I do know that God creates good in everything that happens to His children. There is a purpose for all that happens in our lives, and hopefully it brings people closer to God and to His grace and glory.

Things have happened to me in my life that has obviously affected me in so many ways, but as I walk with the Holy Spirit, Jesus Christ and God, and spend consistent time in the Word of God, I immediately present all my challenges through my prayers to God for His guidance and protection. 1 Corinthians 10:13 states, "No temptation has over-taken you that is not common to man. God is faithful, and he will not let you be tempted beyond your ability, but with the temptation he will also provide the way of escape, that you may be able to endure it." We are to stay faithful in everything whether it is temptation, a challenge in life or a great blessing. God will always show us the path into His purpose in our lives through faith, and for being faithful to God's Word and Jesus Christ. Praise Him.

This is how I truly walk in my truth in Christ. I stay faithful and praise Him no matter what, and keep praying and dwelling in His Word and trusting that He will show me His way in Christ Jesus. I know there will be many challenges and obstacles in my future, but I know that God will never forsake me on my journey and race in Christ, and He will always show me the way out when I am in harm's way. Stay true and faithful to Jesus Christ and He will show you His way.

This is so important, and I will be honest, it is not easy to totally let go of your old self, but the more I let go and get out of the way, and let God in, the more I know I'm walking in my truth in Christ. 1 Thessalonians 5:24 says, "He who calls you is surely faithful, he will surely do it." God is 100% faithful, and has always been 100% faithful to His children. Praise Jesus Christ and is His faithfulness, and walk in your truth in Christ Jesus.

CHAPTER 11

The Fake Out
(Rebuke the Chatter)

This is an important topic for me personally as it has been a continued challenge for me as a believer walking in Christ. I pray for clarity and strength to go through days without hearing negative chatter in my mind. I have become more aware of negative thoughts in my mind, and I am encouraged by the Holy Spirit that the old type of thinking I used to have is now dead. Don't get me wrong, most of the time I am very positive and at peace, and joyful in my heart and mind, but there are moments during some days where the battle still rages inside my mind, as my mind continues to be renewed in the Spirit. The truth is I have no answers that tell exactly how to handle these types of moments in our lives, when our old mind tries to take over and the attack tries to come in. All I can say is to trust in the Lord Jesus Christ with all your heart and to stay focused on the Word of God and His truth. Pray to the Father for His strength, and rebuke or express stern disapproval with your words towards thoughts when they are not in line with the Word of God and His truth about your righteousness in Christ. Cast down every negative thought and stronghold with your words. Mark 4:39-40 states, "And he awoke and rebuked the wind and said to the sea, "Peace! Be still!" And the wind ceased, and there was a great calm. He said to them, "Why are you so afraid? Have you still no faith?" And they were filled with great fear and said to one another, "Who then is this, that even the wind and the sea obey him?""

Remember that as believers we have Christ in us, and we are in Christ, and the resurrection power of the Holy Spirit is in us. We can choose to walk in the authority that Jesus has given to us through the Holy Spirit, through continual faith, and belief, and receive our blessings. Thoughts can circle in our minds and become pervasively worse if they are allowed to fester out of control. We must be proactive and transform to be in tune and aware of our thoughts moving forward in our life in Christ, as the enemy can play tricks on our minds using false suggestions. Sometimes these thoughts can be old thought patterns or memories that must be let go of, as this is our old self. Our old self is dead in Christ, and we are now new creatures in Christ.

Philippians 4:8 states, "Finally brothers, whatever is true, whatever is honorable, whatever is just, whatever is pure, whatever is lovely, whatever is commendable. If there is any excellence, if there is anything worthy of praise, think about these things."

I love this scripture as it touches me in a very powerful way. As I have been mentored by other fellow believers and pastors, this was a scripture that I was brought back to many times, as this truth is what we are to constantly think about in our walk in Christ. Focus on whatever is true in the Word of God, as inspired scripture is the genuine and only truth for us in Christ as a believer. The Holy Spirit will start to give you the gift of discernment so you are able to understand what is true around you and what is not. Be in tune with the Holy Spirit inside you, so you will have the ability and the knowledge to know what is true, or what is not real, or an absolute lie. To think on honorable or positive thought patterns, in regards to what is good and praiseworthy, is so important while moving forward with your life in Christ, because that is what God wants for you. I know that I can personally get caught up in the past, or think about things that I have no control over, or mistakes that I have made in my life, but that's not what the Word of God tells me to do.

The Word of God tells me to think about things that are honorable and whatever is just or right. What does lovely or commendable mean to you? To me, lovely means beautiful or divine and pure, and commendable is something or someone that is praiseworthy. This is where I pray that my thoughts dwell as I mature in Christ. I pray to always remember the truth about the loveliest gift in mankind history, and that is the gift of grace in Jesus Christ and the truth of His Word. Now that is a beautiful thought, and is such a wonderful gift from heaven in the form of the grace of Jesus Christ. If I ever fall back into my old thought patterns of my old self, I am always lifted up out of those thoughts, by dwelling in the Word of God and staying focused on Christ and all the beauty and blessings of my life. I now look to Christ and don't focus on the nonsense that is part of this world that can have an effect on my thoughts. Sometimes this is not easy, but through prayer, faith and Christ in me, I now rebuke them once and for all, as I continue to transform in Christ. It's not me anymore, but Christ in me that is coming out of me. That is where the strength comes from to actually renew my mind. I'm not the one renewing my mind; Christ is doing it through me. Thank you Jesus.

Philippians 4:9 states, "What you have learned and received and heard and seen in me – practice these things and the God of peace will be with you." I believe what the Apostle Paul was saying to us is to notice how he lived His life and mirror Him, and the God of Peace will be with us. Jesus wants us to practice and be obedient to His truths and His peace will be with you and I, as Christ will come out of us through faith. If we live our life in Christ, and Christ in us, Jesus Christ will start to come through us, and permeate out of us as we dwell in His peace. If we live a life that isn't in Christ or like Christ, then we will be swayed away from His true peace which is not in His true purpose for us.

1 Corinthians 2:16 states, "For who has understood the mind of the Lord so as to instruct him? But we have the mind of Christ and do hold the thoughts of his heart." This powerful scripture tells us a significant truth in the fact that Paul says we have the mind of Jesus Christ our Lord and Savior. Imagine that! In Christ we have the mind of Christ and hold the thoughts of His heart in our minds. Why do we still hold onto thoughts of anxiousness, doubts, and certain types of old thought patterns that is definitely not the mind of Christ? I am not sure exactly why we still fall back into old thoughts, but I believe that this is part of our transformation process and the process of renewing our minds in Christ. In this life through Christ and His grace, we will have more and more thoughts like Christ as His Spirit is coming out of us more and more every day. In heaven we will truly not have any thoughts that aren't of Christ and His love for us. I will say that as we are living in our truth in Christ, we should focus on Christ's love for us, and on the fact that we are His, as He purchased all of us for the ultimate price. It is over, and we are in Christ through grace, once and for all, if we believe and have faith in Jesus Christ as our Lord and Savior.

Matthew 21:21-22 states, "And Jesus answered them, truly I say to you, if you have faith and do not doubt, you will not only do what has been done to the fig tree, but even if you say to this mountain, be taken up and thrown into the sea, it will happen. And whatever you ask in prayer, you will receive, if you have faith." Doubting is a choice and it's a result of the fake out from the incorrect way of thinking and walking in our new identity in Christ. For those of you who are in Christ, and saved through the blood of Jesus Christ, I want to encourage you to let go, through prayer and His strength, any doubts about your justification and life in Christ. Accept it fully, and I believe that your life and thoughts will change in a positive Christ like way. Let go of your old self. Just let go. Your faith comes from God and you don't have to build up faith, but it is given to you through Jesus Christ, from God in heaven, if you receive it. Believe or don't believe it, but that's what the Word of God says, so if you have made the choice to believe, then accept your measure of faith that God has given to you and move mountains in your life through Christ, not your own will power. All of those old thoughts, doubts, and feelings of pain and the lack of self worth can now be thrown into the sea, if you ask in prayer, you will receive. You must not only have faith, which is a gift, but you must act on your faith and not on your doubt by believing with all your heart and mind. Jesus Christ has already done everything for you, so believe in this truth of grace and receive it once and for all with authority.

Matthew 6:25-34 states, "Therefore I tell you, do not be anxious about your life, what you will eat or what you will drink, nor about your body, what you will put on. Is not life more than food and the body more than clothing? Look at the birds of the air; they neither sow nor reap nor gather into barns, and yet your heavenly Father feeds them. Are you not of more value than they? And which of you by being anxious can add a single hour to his span of life? And why are you anxious about clothing? Consider the lilies of the field, how they grow; they neither toil nor spin, yet I tell you, even Solomon in all his glory was not arrayed like one of these. But if God so clothes the grass of the field, which today is alive and tomorrow is thrown into the oven, will he not much more clothe you, O you of little faith? Therefore do not be anxious, saying what shall we eat? Or what shall we drink? Or what shall we wear? For the Gentiles seek after all these things, and your heavenly Father knows that you need them all. But seek first the kingdom of God and his righteousness, and all these things will be added to you. Therefore do not be anxious about tomorrow, for tomorrow will be anxious for itself. Sufficient for the day is its own trouble."

My brothers and sisters in Christ, who are reading this book, I say to you that anxiety had been one of the biggest strongholds of my old self, but Christ and the Holy Spirit has renewed me and transformed me through grace to overcome it. People are always looking for miracles. Well I can truly say that Jesus has set me free from constant anxieties in my life, which is one of the biggest miracles of my life in Christ. I had been at a war in my mind fighting anxieties for years, but one of the greatest gifts that I've been blessed with in Christ is I now have victory over anxiety. You know what the Word of God and the Holy Trinity has shown and integrated into me? *The Word of God tells me that the battle has already been won by Jesus Christ.* How can I be fighting a battle that's already been won by Christ? Wow! This has been the ultimate fake out for me from the enemy and my old self. I had been trying to fight a stronghold by myself that has already been defeated, and is over. That would be like going to play in a sporting event, walking out on the field, and the game is already over. You and I have already won, because Christ has already won the battle for us. *Game over!*

If we are still fighting a battle that's already over, that doesn't make sense, does it? No, it doesn't to me. This is why I know that one of biggest lies that the enemy tells us is that the battle has not been won. It's the biggest ultimate fake out for the believer or the non-believer from the enemy. Don't believe it? The battle has been won by Jesus Christ on Calvary. One thing I know about living in this world is that sin has been multiplying since Adam and Eve, but sin was defeated by Jesus Christ once and for all, for those who believe and are in Christ through grace. I have now accepted all my blessings and the strength to let go of the walking dead of my old life, that still tries to peek its ugly head out every once in a while. *I'm over it.* I pray and accept Jesus Christ's thoughts to renew and fill my mind every second of my life. I pray for all of you, that your minds are filled in Christ, and that the entire fake out regarding the battle still waging will be gone from your life. If attacked, then you immediately will know to rebuke those thoughts with your words with authority in Christ. Amen.

It is written in Romans 8:5-7, "For those who live according to the flesh set their minds on the things of the flesh; but those who live according to the Spirit set their minds on the things of the Spirit. For to set the mind on the flesh is death, but to set the mind on the Spirit is life and peace. For the mind that is set on the flesh is hostile to God, for it does not submit to God's law; indeed, it cannot." This should be the standard and foundation that our minds must focus on. Our thoughts should stay centered on God, Jesus Christ and the Holy Spirit, and through the Holy Spirit we will be given discernment so we can have life and have peace of mind. If we are going to set our minds on fleshly things of this world, then that is against God, for it does not submit to God's law, as it can't because it doesn't have an understanding and obedience to the things of the Spirit. Pray for strength as you are righteous and bold in Christ, as you now have the ability in Christ to walk that way. The more you walk in Christ, and the more you dwell on things of the Holy Spirit, Christ, and His Word, the more your mind will be continually renewed to have the mind of Christ. Glory in Christ.

John 8:31-32 states, "So Jesus said to the Jews who had believed in him, If you abide in my word, you are truly my disciples, and you will know the truth and the truth will set you free." Jesus states for all of us who are "truly" His disciples that we will know His truth and we will know not only in our spirit and soul but in our minds. We will be set free by His truth. It's is critical moving forward with your truth in Christ to abide or dwell in the Word of God. This is absolutely mandatory for peace in your life, for the believer to be in prayer and spend quality time in the Word and with God, and make these things a top priority in their lives every day. This is the truth, not the fake out.

Psalm 1:1-2 states, "Blessed is the man who walks not in the counsel of the wicked, nor stands in the way of sinners, nor sits in the seat of scoffers; but his delight is in the law of the Lord, and on his law he meditates day and night." It is written in Romans 12:2, "Do not be conformed to this world, but be transformed by the renewal of your mind that by tasting you may discern what is the will of God, what is good and acceptable and perfect." This is awesome. This answers the question to me about how we will know what is right. Paul states to not be conformed to this world as we are not from this world, as we are now a part of the kingdom of God in Christ. Paul says that our minds must be renewed or transformed or changed by tasting or trying different things, so that through the Holy Spirit and Christ we can have discernment. In Christ we will now be able to tell the difference between what is in the Spirit and what is fleshly, and by this truth we will know what God's will is for us. To walk in our truth in Christ we must know what God's will is for us. We will be able to separate between what we should be doing compared to what we shouldn't be doing. This is vital to walking in our truth in Christ.

Romans 8:26 states, "Likewise the Spirit helps us in our weakness. For we do not know what to pray for as we ought, but the Spirit himself intercedes for us with groaning too deep for words." I love this because some days I just don't understand what's happening to me or around me. Don't you ever feel that way? Paul says that the Holy Spirit is praying or interceding for us with groans too deep for words. Can you imagine that? I thank you Jesus and thank you Holy Spirit for this gift. Wow. Thank you Father God. Sometimes I don't know what to pray for, but I now know that the Holy Spirit, who knows everything about me and my thoughts, is interceding and praying to God for me which brings me a peace that is so far beyond what I ever thought peace was.

It is written in Romans 8:28, "And we know that for those who love God all things work together for good, for those who are called according to his purpose." I love God, how about you? Yes, I hope and pray that everyone loves and has a relationship with God, Jesus Christ, and the Holy Spirit. I know that everything works in concert together for good in Christ Jesus. I want to be kind, loving, and encourage people, and I know that is why God has given me this gift and the inspiration to write these words. I wouldn't have had a clue on my own how to formulate these words, but in Christ, all things are possible for good for those who are called according to His purpose. This is huge in what we are talking about. *Walking in our truth in Christ is not about us, it's about walking in unison with Christ for His purpose and His glory.* That means that when we are walking in our truth in Christ, we are doing God's will and His purpose for us, for His glory. Nothing can keep you from your purpose in Christ as it's the Father's purpose for you. Do you love people? This is number one to God. Love people with all your heart in Christ as you walk in your truth in Christ, and rebuke the chatter in your mind that isn't in line with His Word. I encourage all of you to go and walk in God's will for your life which is love, peace, and rest for His glory.

CHAPTER 12

Love like Christ

It is written in Deuteronomy 6:5, "You shall love the Lord your God with all your heart and with all your soul and with all your might." When talking about love, we should start with how much we love the Lord our God with all our heart, and with all our soul, and with all our might. Basically to me, that means with everything I have, and with every fiber of my being, without holding back at all. In truth, God gives me His love through Christ, to love Him with all that He has given to me in Christ. I pray we all love God, the Lord Jesus Christ, and the Holy Spirit, with everything we have eternally in Christ, and through Christ, and with as much power as we can pray for in Christ. In Christ we can love God in a way that only God can love. Pray for this gift of God's love showing up in your lives. Let's all love God with everything we have, but remember if we are in Christ, then we have Christ love, so let's love with everything that Christ has given to us through His grace.

Matthew 22:37–39 states, "And he said to them you shall love the Lord your God with all your heart and with all your soul and with all your mind. This is the great and first commandment. And a second is like it: You shall love your neighbor as yourself." In Christ and through Christ, your life can now be a reflection of the Lord Jesus Christ, God, and the Holy Spirit, and will be about shining that love onto other people. The Holy Spirit transforms us from the old self that we used to be, to our new truth in Jesus Christ. It's about loving God, Christ, and the Holy Spirit, and sharing that love with other people that we come in contact with in our lives.

It is written in 1 John 4:7-12, "Beloved, let us love one another, for love is from God, and whoever loves has been born of God and knows God. Anyone who does not love does not know God, because God is love. In this the love of God was made manifest among us, that God sent his only son into the world, so that we might live through him. In this is love, not that we have loved God but that he loved us and sent his son to be the propitiation for our sins. Beloved, if God so loved us, we also ought to love one another. If we love one another, God abides in us and His love is perfected in us."

Only because we are in Christ can we ever aspire to love like Christ. Remember the fact that once you are a child of God in Christ through faith, He has given His fruits and His love to us so we can truly love like Christ. Dwell and meditate on this truth. Christ coming out of the believer is what enables the believer to love like Christ. This is critical in moving forward with our walk in Christ, to believe and to know in our heart that there is no pressure on us as believers. Our focus is to believe, and walk in our identity in Christ, and trust in God's truth for our life. *It is Christ coming out of us in every aspect of our being that will bring the believer to that place where we are now walking in Christ, in us and through us, so we are in His peace, rest and love.* What a beautiful truth this is to be in Christ's rest, love, and peace for us as His family. I ask you to open up your heart and mind as you push through the rest of this book to explore what Christ has in store for you in Him. Truth in Christ is about what Christ is, and always has been doing in our lives, and what He will continue to do through us. Christ holds our lives together right now. He is and has always been faithful.

1 John 4:16-21 states, "So we have come to know and to believe the love that God has for us. God is love, and whoever abides in love abides in God, and God abides in him. By this is love perfected with us, so that we may have confidence for the Day of Judgment because as He is so also are we in this world. There is no fear in love, but perfect love casts out fear. For fear has to do with punishment, and whoever fears has not been perfected in love. We love because he first loved us. If anyone says, 'I love God,' and hates his brother whom he has seen cannot love God whom he has not seen. And this commandment we have from him; whoever loves God must also love his brother."

When we have accepted Christ as our Lord and Savior, we have come to know His perfect love for us and what Jesus Christ sacrificed for us, so we can live in Christ through grace which is Christ. To truly grasp what God did for us in offering up His Son for us, as sinners of this world, so we could have everlasting life in Christ is hard to imagine. I have a son named Luke and a daughter named Mariah, and I know what that would mean to me. It would be like dying for me to lose my child the way Christ was given up for us. Think about this enormous sacrifice by God before moving on with this book. *Grace was not free as it came at the ultimate price through the blood of Jesus Christ.*

Think about just how much God loves you and exactly what He did for your sins. Now that is ultimate love. Never forget just how much God has done for you, including the fact that He created every aspect of your life, and of all those who have ever lived, and everything that has ever been created. God has given us the covenant of grace so we will not be separated from Him anymore, in Christ and through Christ. God's love for us is infinite. There is no end to the love that God, Christ, and the Holy Spirit has for us through faith in His Son Jesus Christ. It is God's nature to be loving and graceful towards His children in Christ.

God's Word says that God is love, and whoever abides in love abides in God through Christ as Christ abides in God. Our love is now perfected in Christ, and through Christ, so that His love is now ours for those who believe and receive His love. We now have confidence to know that Christ's love is in us. Let go of the way you used to believe that you loved people. If you are in Christ, your love will be a different type of love, because it's not your love anymore, its Jesus Christ's love coming through you, and out of you, towards the people around you. The Word of God says that we should be confident in this, because as Christ is, so also are we in this world. God sees you as He sees Christ when you are in Christ and believe through grace. We will talk more about this in the next chapter, but the Word of God says there is no fear in love, but perfect love, which is Christ's love, casts out fear and throws it all away. Christ's love is the way to have true peace in your life. Dwell in it right now. The only reason we love is because God first loved us, and if we truly know God through Christ, we will love and forgive our brothers and sisters no matter what. Our love is perfected in Christ for all to share with us in our lives. Let out the love that is in you through Christ because it's perfect, so forgive others, and forgive yourself in Christ. 2 Chronicles 5:14 states, "For his steadfast love endures forever."

1 Corinthians 13:1-13 states, "If I speak in the tongues of men and of angels, but have not love, I am a noisy gong or a clanging cymbal. And if I have prophetic powers, and understand all mysteries and all

knowledge, and if I have all faith, so as to remove mountains, but have not love, I am nothing. If I give away all I have, and if I deliver up my body to burned, but have not love, I gain nothing. Love is patient and kind; love does not envy or boast; it is not arrogant or rude. It does not insist on its own way; it is not irritable or resentful; it does not rejoice at wrongdoing, but rejoices with the truth. Love bears all things, believes all things, hopes all things, and endures all things. Love never ends. As for prophecies, they will pass away; as for tongues, they will cease; as for knowledge, it will pass away. For we know in part and we prophesy in part, but when the perfect comes, the partial will pass away. When I was a child, I spoke like a child. When I became a man, I gave up childish ways. For now we see in a mirror dimly, but then face to face. Now I know in part; then I shall know fully, even as I have been fully known. So now faith, hope, and love abide, these three; but the greatest of these is love."

In this scripture we learn that without love in our lives we are nothing. Think about it. If we don't love others, then truly we must ask ourselves, how can Christ be in us? If we are in Christ, we will love others and there is nothing that can ever stop this truth. Christ's love will come out of us as believers, in His way, not in our old ways. This truth creates so much joy in me. As I walk in my truth in Christ, His love will flow from every element of my life.

To have the faith to move mountains and not love is a huge statement. I don't see how you could have one without the other, but God's Word is making a strong point, that love is everything and it must be the foundation in our lives as a believer; in fact it must be our greatest fruit that is being manifested in us who believe. Scripture explains what love in our lives actually looks like. The first thing the Word states is that love is patient and love is kind. I think we all know what both of these words mean, but I would say that we need to take a look at our lives to see if we are really patient or enduring or long suffering with others in our lives. To be kind or gentle with others is a strong outward manifestation of our love for others. It will be apparent in how we interact with others around us, and it's so nice to be around gentle and kind people in my life.

How about being kind and patient with our own self? This is an important topic that we must discuss moving forward, and that's the obvious truth that to love, is not just about loving others, but it's about how much we love God, Jesus Christ, the Holy Spirit, and our own self. This can be tough sometimes, but we must take a closer look at this in the next chapter. Love does not envy or isn't jealous or doesn't boast. This truth tells me that true love does not have to be anything except what it is with someone. When we truly love someone it doesn't need to have stipulations or conditions, plus there is a trust apparent within that love for someone. It also tells me that we don't need to sing our own praises about the relationship, or about ourselves. If we are blessed to love someone in any circumstance, then we should be thankful for the experience of love, especially God's love in us coming out.

What a gift it is to love someone and actually be loved back. Love is never arrogant or conceited or rude. Basically there should be nothing negative about your love for others in Christ. Those characteristics are ugly and should never be associated with love especially when in Christ. Our love, not being insistent in our own way, is a vast topic in itself. I could probably write a whole book on this topic alone. But consider how many times, in a relationship or friendship, we try to get things done in our own way. This kind of behavior is not love, but is selfish.

Psalm 145:8 states, "The Lord is gracious and merciful, slow to anger and abounding in steadfast love." Without the grace of our Lord and Savior Jesus Christ, we are separated from God and His perfect love, but with His grace we are alive in Christ, and forgiven in Christ, as He shows us His mercy in every way of life. The Lord is patient with His children in every way. I am thankful that the Lord is slow to anger towards me even when I fall short in my life. I know I am saved in Jesus Christ, and I am justified by His grace. I thank you Father, that you see your children like you see your Son Jesus. I am dwelling in Jesus Christ's abounding and steadfast love, but to now know that God is always abounding in love towards His children, through Jesus Christ, brings me peace and rest especially when things get tough or challenging in my life. My brothers and sisters, please take the time to realize this truth that the Lord is always there for you, and loves you more than you can ever imagine or I could ever explain. Jesus wants to be the most important part of our lives, as He is always merciful, steadfast, and consistently loving toward us.

Micah 6:8 states, "He has told you, O man what is good; and what does the Lord require of you but to do justice, and to love kindness, and to walk humbly with your God." Let us walk in kindness towards others in our walk and truth in Christ, and this includes everyone that we come in contact with, to love and enjoy kindness. Jesus Christ was and continues to be the picture of kindness for all mankind for all eternity. Let us be humble and kind in everything we do, knowing that our Lord is always there in our lives to bring us His gifts and strengths for His glory. We should be constantly striving to be fair in everything we do, with everyone we come in contact with. Jesus is the prime example of how to live our lives, and how to treat others. Let us humbly go through life, knowing that God has given us everlasting life and everything in it. It's not about you or I, it's about Christ and His glory shining through us and out of us. God has blessed every aspect of our lives. In Christ, receive it, and then we share it with others.

In Matthew 5:44-48 Jesus tells us, "But I say to you, Love your enemies and pray for those who persecute you, so that you may be sons of your Father who is in heaven. For he makes his sun rise on the evil and on the good and sends rain on the just and on the unjust. For if you love those who love you, what reward do you have? Do not even the tax collectors do the same? And if you greet only your brothers, what more are you doing than others? Do not even the Gentiles do the same? You therefore must be perfect, as your heavenly Father is perfect." To me it seems that Jesus wants all who are in Him to pray for everyone, not just the loved ones in our lives, but to pray for and love everyone. I know that I can only be perfect in Christ as He is perfect.

It is written in Romans 12: 9-21, "Let love be genuine. Abhor what is evil; hold fast to what is good. Love one another with brotherly affection. Outdo one another in showing honor. Do not be slothful in zeal, be fervent in spirit, and serve the Lord. Rejoice in hope, be patient in tribulation, be constant in prayer. Contribute to the needs of the saints and seek to show hospitality. Bless those who persecute you; bless and do not curse them. Rejoice with those who rejoice, weep with those who weep. Live in harmony with one another. Do not be haughty, but associate with the lowly. Never be wise in your own sight. Repay no one evil for evil, but give thought to do what is honorable in the sight of all. If possible, so far as it depends on you, live peaceably with all. Beloved, never avenge yourselves, but leave it to the wrath of God, for it is written, "vengeance is mine, I will repay, says the Lord. To the contrary, if your enemy is hungry, feed him; if he is thirsty, give him something to drink; for by so doing you will heap burning coals on his head. Do not be overcome by evil, but overcome evil with good."

Everyone is always looking for a manual or a road map for life. This truth lays it out precisely for all of us. This is the way to live our lives, and to share Christ's love with others. Christ has conquered everything in life, and our lives through Christ should be a testimony of Christ in us. Let's take every opportunity that God brings to our lives to love people and to treat them as Christ has loved and treated us. To walk in truth in Christ is to love all people, like Christ has loved us all, unconditionally and with grace. What a blessing it is to have Christ's love in us, so that we can share that love with others in our lives, plus people that we don't know. *Christ's love is perfect love and it is now in us who believe.*

CHAPTER 13

Be Reconciled with Yourself through Christ Because God is Reconciled with You In Christ

Let's discuss how you can let go of everything you have ever done wrong, including all your past sins, once and for all, if you are in Christ, and Christ is in you and lives through you right now. In Christ, God sees you and me as completely righteous and perfect. We are now reconciled with God through grace if you are in Christ. This has been, and is still sometimes hard for me to fully understand, but as I become more enlightened to the truth about grace, I now fully embrace that I am now reconciled with God, right now in Christ Jesus, for which I am so thankful. I have been brought back into fellowship with God, as I was once alienated from God through the sinful nature that I was born into, but now I'm under the covenant of grace.

Let's take a deeper look at this truth and how it can bring us to a deeper Christ-like peace in our lives, and free us to move forward with understanding and thankfulness. Now I walk in the truth that Jesus Christ has freed me from condemnation once and for all, because of His grace on me, and receiving Him as my Lord and Savior. I was meditating and praying about this, and I started to become more joyful and truly thankful that I am in fact at peace with God through Christ. Here is what I realized. I hadn't yet let go of my old sins in regards to being reconciled with myself and my past. I was still convicted in myself about my past, but then it hit me. God has forgiven me, as I am now reconciled to Him through my belief in Jesus Christ. I prayed for a revelation in my heart to now forgive myself and let go of all my past, present and future sins. Let's take a look at what the scripture says about reconciliation, and continue our discussion about being reconciled with ourselves in Christ.

It is written in 2 Corinthians 5:18-21, "All this is from God, who through Christ reconciled us to himself and gave us the ministry of reconciliation; that is, in Christ, God was reconciling the world to himself, not counting their trespasses against them, and entrusting to us the message of reconciliation. Therefore, we are ambassadors for Christ, God making his appeal through us. We implore you on behalf of Christ, be reconciled to God. For our sake he made him to be sin who knew no sin, so that in him we might become the righteousness of God." Everything is from God through Christ. The scripture clearly states that through Christ we, who believe in Christ Jesus as our Lord and Savior, are now reconciled to God. Jesus Christ has now given us the ministry of reconciliation once and for all, for those who believe in Christ Jesus because of Him being their Lord and Savior and because of His grace. We have now been entrusted with this message. Therefore we are now 'Ambassadors for Christ,' while we are alive. God is making

His appeal through believers. For mankind's sake, God made Jesus to be sinful, who had never known sin, so that in Him we might become the righteousness of God. So let's think about this for a second. *Through Christ we are now the righteousness of God.* Through grace, God sees us who believe in Jesus Christ, like He sees His only Son. Through grace we are now clean and pure just as Christ is. This is absolutely incredible to me, that in Christ, I am now forgiven of all my past, present, and future sins, as Jesus Christ is my propitiation for my life. He took my place. This is incredible! This is God's grace and mercy on those who believe. Stop and thank the Lord Jesus Christ for this incredible gift of grace and reconciliation with God the Father.

It is written in Romans 5:10-11, "For if while we were enemies we were reconciled to God by the death of his Son, much more, now that we are reconciled, shall we be saved by his life. More than that, we also rejoice in God through our Lord Jesus Christ, through whom we have now received reconciliation." In this scripture, it talks about how when we were not in Christ, we were enemies with God. To me, that is the worst place to be in life and not where I wanted to be. I am so thankful that through the death and resurrection of His Son Jesus Christ, I am saved, reconciled, justified, and no longer God's enemy, as I am now covered by the blood Jesus Christ through faith. We should be so thankful and joyful that we, who believe in Jesus Christ as our Lord and Savior, have now received reconciliation with the Father and the creator of life. We have been adopted into the family of God through our Lord and Savior Jesus Christ. Thank you Jesus.

Colossians 1:21-23 states, "And you, who once were alienated and hostile in mind, doing evil deeds, he has now reconciled in his body of flesh by his death, in order to present you holy and blameless and above reproach before him, if indeed you continue in the faith, stable and steadfast, not shifting from the hope of the gospel that you heard, which has been proclaimed in all creation under heaven, and of which I, Paul, became a minister." We must continue in the faith, stable and steadfast, not shifting from the hope of the gospel that we have heard which has been proclaimed in all creation under heaven.

It is written in Hebrews 9:26 states, "For then he would have had to suffer repeatedly since the foundation of the world. But as it is, he has appeared once for all at the end of the ages to put away sin by the sacrifice of himself." Christ sacrificed Himself for all who believe in Him. This scripture really moved me when I was thinking about this truth about reconciling myself in Christ. If I don't forgive myself and God has forgiven me through Christ, what is that saying about my faith, and what Jesus did for me, and for all those who believe? I have committed so many sins in my life. I wasn't even recognizing certain elements of my life that was in sin, but I knew I had a lot of sin in my life. It was very hard for me to let it go and forgive myself, and I was drowning in my old sins, even though I believed that Jesus had died for my sins. Through the Holy Spirit and prayer, Christ has given me the understanding and discernment, through the truth of the scripture, that I can let go of my old sins once and for all, and so can you.

If God sees me as perfect, then why can't I see myself as perfect? The truth is, I can, and I now do through faith, because Jesus Christ shed His blood for you and me, who believe in Him as our Lord and Savior. What would give me the thought that I can't let go of my old sins since God has forgiven me and reconciled me with Himself through His Son Jesus? Being justified in Christ is my new identity in Christ, and any other thoughts to the contrary are again a fake out, either from the enemy or my old self. I believe that Jesus Christ, who never knew sin, became sin, so I could be reconciled with God through faith. There is absolutely no reason in Christ why I can't be reconciled to myself once and for all, and truly be able to rest in His peace and walk in His truth, and there is no reason why you can't as well. This truth has been one of my biggest revelations as a believer in Christ and has truly set me free.

It is written in Ephesians 2:16-22, "And might reconcile us both to God in one body through the cross, thereby killing the hostility. And he came and preached peace to you who were far off and peace to those who were near. For through him we both have access in one Spirit to the Father. So then you are no longer strangers and aliens, but you are fellow citizens with the saints and members of the household of God, built on the foundation of the apostles and prophets, Christ Jesus himself being the cornerstone, in whom the whole structure, being joined together, grows in a holy temple in the Lord. In him you also are being built together into a dwelling place for God by the Spirit." We are now members of the household of God, in one body, through the cross, with no more hostility. Believers are not slaves to sin anymore in Christ. We are no longer outcasts or strangers or aliens, but we are part of God's family. *Every blessing in Christ is now our identity through Jesus Christ as the adopted children of God.* This truth is built on the solid foundation of the apostles and prophets, and the Word of God through Jesus Christ. Our Lord Jesus Christ is the cornerstone in which the entire structure is joined together, as everything goes in and through Jesus Christ. In Him we are also being built together into a dwelling place for God by the Holy Spirit. We are now a part of the body of Christ, in Christ, for God's glory.

Jesus said in Mark 10:45, "For even the Son of Man came not to be served but to serve, and to give his life as a ransom for many." Let's go full circle with this for a minute and talk about what I was dealing with in the beginning of this chapter- being reconciled with God through

Christ because of the ultimate ransom that Christ paid for me and my sins. This truth is a blessing for me, as it is grace in its purest form because I didn't deserve it. Jesus came down to Earth to serve, not to be served, and He is glorified by God. Jesus gave His life for you and I, who believe, so we could be reconciled to the Father. Again, Wow! What gives me the thought that I can't be reconciled to myself for all my sins, and yet believe that I am reconciled by God? This is a lie from the enemy; I constantly pray for strength and continued discernment to know the truth of the Word of God, and have the understanding that not only am I reconciled through Christ with God, but I am also reconciled to my new self as a new creature in Christ. I needed to finally let go of my old self and all the guilt and shame, and move forward in my new life in Christ Jesus, and the truth of His Word through faith in Jesus Christ. We can all truly walk in our truth in Christ, when we realize we are truly reconciled to God through Christ and walk as a new creation in our Lord and Savior. Be blessed and praise Him and glorify Him, and through Christ reconcile yourself to your new self, and don't look back. *Look to Jesus and push through your 'old self' to your new identity in Christ.*

CHAPTER 14

God Has Called You into His Peace (So Rest in His Peace)

It is written in 1 Corinthians 7:15, "God has called you to peace." God has called me, and all who believe, to dwell and rest in the peace of Christ through Christ. First off, let's discuss what it means to be called. God has called me, which means God is expecting and authorizing me to live in the peace that Christ brings to my life. I now have a bridge of faith in Christ to walk and live in the peace of Christ for my life. This place of Christ's peace is where we are now as believers, if we truly accept all the blessings of the Lord in our lives. Meditate on this truth. God has called you, if you are in Christ, to have the peace of the Lord Jesus Christ over all your life, and to share this peace with others. This is incredible, and a powerful truth for all of us who believe, but we need to make the choice to believe and seize this truth.

Peace creates harmony in our minds, hearts, body, and spirits, and I truly believe the only way to find this peace is to be in Christ. It's Christ' peace in us. If I were to say that I am in total peace every day of my life, that would not be true, but I do know that if for any reason I find myself out of Christ's peace due to the forces of this world, I know where to look, and to re-engage my peace, and that is right in the Word of God, and focus on Jesus Christ and pray to Him. These times show me that I may have turned away, or become distracted from my true source of peace, which is in Christ Jesus. God's purpose for me is to have the peace of Christ flowing through me at all times, then out of me towards others through faith in Jesus Christ. The only way to stay in Christ's peace is to keep my focus on Jesus Christ, and be in the Word of God at all times, and to realize that Christ is flowing through me through the Holy Spirit. I have come to a place of accepting that my peace has nothing to do with what I do, but with what Christ has already done for me, and for me to live and walk in this truth.

It is written in Romans 5:1, "Therefore, since we have been justified by faith, we have peace with God through our Lord Jesus Christ. Through him we have also obtained access by faith into this grace in which we stand, and we rejoice in hope of the glory of God." I am so thankful and I want to praise Jesus again. I know I keep saying it, but I truly am thankful for the mercy and grace of God through Jesus Christ in my life. I won't hold back anymore in my worship and my love towards my Father in heaven, my Lord and Savior Jesus Christ, and the Holy Spirit who dwells in me. Praise you Father God, Jesus Christ, and the Holy Spirit. Thank you.

We have already talked about being righteous in Christ, which means believers are now looked at by God as pure and without sin, but this scripture also shares with us that we have peace with our God, where before Christ we were in sin, and those who were under the law were bound by the law. In Christ, through grace, we now have complete access to God through prayer and Jesus Christ. If you are in Christ, you can have the greatest peace you've ever imagined, and that's peace with God. Now that's true peace. The only way to start to comprehend this truth is to walk with the Lord every second of every day. The Holy Spirit will give you peace and He will also give you discernment of how incredible a gift this actually is. Embrace this truth in Christ. Christ's peace for your life.

It is written in Philippians 4:7, "And the peace of God, which surpasses all understanding, will guard your hearts and your minds in Christ Jesus." The beauty of this truth is that we might not ever fully understand what it means to have the peace of God, because it surpasses all of our understanding, but this peace will guard and protect our hearts and minds in Christ Jesus. I always find myself trying to understand things, and I am starting to learn and trust to just let it go, and utilize the faith that God has given to me through Jesus Christ and the Holy Spirit, and let go of the idea of controlling my life. God is in control of my life through Jesus Christ in me. My choice is to be in Christ through faith. Numbers 6:26 states, "The Lord lift up his countenance upon you and give you peace." The peace we experience as a believer in Christ is the peace of Christ, but we must be open for this peace to take hold of our lives and to let go of our old self and rest. God does His best work when we get out of the way and just rest and be held by the love of Christ. In fact, when we start trying to do things that we think will bring us peace, it can possibly get in the way of Christ's peace having complete effect on us.

Luke 1:79 states, "To give light to those who sit in darkness and in the shadow of death, to guide our feet into the way of peace." Through the peace of Christ, God is giving us light, where before we were walking and living in darkness and in the shadow of death and continual sin. The Father is now guiding our walk into the way of peace which is in

Christ Jesus. As I write this, it is stirring my heart, and I am looking back at just how much Christ has guided my walk into His light and out of the darkness in every aspect of my life. Now that I am in Christ, and His light is shining out of me towards others, I can truly see it strongly in other believers. Grace is so abundant in Christ that it will overflow from us to others so we can share the love and peace of Christ with all people. It pours out of us believers so we become lights in Christ, for Christ.

This light is the way to peace and love through Christ. Psalm 34:14 states, "Turn away from evil and do good; seek peace and pursue it." God wants us to turn away from all that is evil and do incredible things through the power of the Holy Spirit and Jesus Christ. He wants us to fully understand the peace of Christ, and to rest in His peace. To me, that is telling me that whenever I am not in Christ's peace, I should be turning towards Christ, because there is always peace in Christ. If I am not in peace, then I have something distracting me from Christ, like a stronghold or an idol in my heart, or I have created an idea of my life that is interfering with Christ's peace. I will be honest with all of you. This happens to me some days, and I would venture to say it happens to most people, even believers, as this is truly part of the good fight which we are walking in. We are being transformed to be like Christ, so keep praying and praising God for the peace that He has already given to you. Receive it, walk in it, pursue it, and run after it in your lives.

John 14:27 Jesus tells us, "Peace I leave with you; my peace I give to you. Not as the world gives do I give to you. Let not your hearts be troubled, neither let them be afraid." Through the Holy Spirit, Christ gives us His peace and plants it in us, and it is given freely by God to those who are in Christ so we don't need to be fearful anymore. Let us dwell in this truth as we live our lives, and know that our flesh may fight this truth, but our spirit knows the real truth. I am reminded by the Holy Spirit to be focused on Jesus Christ and God at all times. The Word of God is the truth that I can hold on to when I am feeling uneasy about anything. God doesn't want us to be troubled about anything, as we are His heirs and His children in Christ. I could probably write a book about this truth alone, and I pray that you will all dwell on this scripture always. When we live our truth in Christ, His peace will manifest itself into our lives. As Isaiah 9:6 states, "For to us a child is born, to us a son is given; and the government shall be upon his shoulder and his name shall be called Wonderful Counselor, Mighty God, Everlasting Father, Prince of Peace." Christ is our Prince of Peace for eternity as we are His, purchased by His blood. Rest in His peace as Jesus is the Prince of Peace in our lives, and focus all of your prayers and thoughts on His peace that is in you right this minute if you are in Christ. His peace is now our peace, as we walk in Christ.

John 16:33 tell us, "I have said these things to you, that in me you may have peace. In the world you will have tribulation. But take heart; I have overcome the world." If we focus on the world and our fleshly needs and desires, this peace will be affected, and there can be tribulation and trials, but it doesn't have to be like this. This is the sinful world that we live in, but it's not where we have to be, as we are not a part of this world anymore in Christ. Jesus Christ has overcome this world, and the sin and death of humanity, and our Lord has given us a new way, a new truth for us to dwell in. When things are going bad, and I know they can, please take hold of this truth always and pray for mercy and for God to wash away any stronghold that is holding on to you, and praise our Lord and Savior Jesus Christ. There is peace in Christ, so rest in it, and dwell and remember always that God has called you into His peace through our Lord and Savior Jesus Christ.

It is written in Romans 8:6, "For to set the mind on the flesh is death, but to set the mind on the Spirit is life and peace." This scripture tells me that the battle of peace dwells in our minds. This scripture tells us to set our thoughts and our minds on Jesus Christ, His Word, God, and the Holy Spirit will discern His truth into our lives, and this will bring us life and Christ's peace into our lives. But if we constantly focus our minds on effects of the flesh and of this world, it will only bring us death and strife. This is really important for dwelling in your truth in Christ. I encourage all believers to take authority over your thoughts and stay focused on the truth of the Word of God. That's why it's so important to spend as much time as possible in His Word. Scripture is God talking to us through His Word, while the Holy Spirit gives us a discernment to comprehend what God is sharing with us, so we can manifest this truth into our daily lives. This is our new truth as a new creation in Christ. Living in our truth in Christ means to dwell on God's truth, not on the things of this world. It is written in Ephesians 6:15, "And as shoes for your feet, having put on the readiness given by the gospel of peace." You are now equipped in Christ to dwell in His peace for eternity.

Colossians 3:15 states, "And let the peace of Christ rule in your hearts, to which indeed you were called in one body. And be thankful." Those of us who believe in Jesus Christ were called into one body, the body of our Lord and Savior Jesus Christ. We were appointed and called to dwell in Christ's love forever and ever. I know I've said 'wow' in this commentary a lot, but I am completely amazed at the grace of God, Jesus Christ, and the Holy Spirit that they would call me to His perfect body through faith in Jesus Christ, even before I was born. Paul tells us to "Let the peace of Christ rule in our hearts," which implies and tells me that we may be getting in the way. I have sometimes been guilty of this because of me trying to control things. Control had been an idol of mine and it took me away from focusing and trusting God with every aspect of my life, even though I knew Jesus knows of every hair on my head. Jesus has transformed this part of my life which is another miracle of my life. *I have finally let go of the stronghold of control and I'm letting the peace of God rule my life. Thank you Jesus.*

When we accept Christ in our hearts, and into our lives, we are saying that we believe in all His truths and God's love for us, and that we want Jesus to take over our lives and come through us. Please, let's all get out of the way and pray that we can trust to let the peace of Christ rule in our hearts as we live our lives in Christ, and walk in our truth in Christ. As I transform in my life in Christ, I can still lose my peace sometimes, but the Holy Spirit makes me instantly aware of it when it happens, and I immediately go to the Word of God and pray, and I am brought back into God's peace. Let's pray to Christ together. *I pray to Jesus Christ that I have received all of your peace in all aspects of my life moving forward, as I truly have let go. I pray to receive all your peace as it reigns in my heart, and rules my life through Jesus Christ. I pray always in the name of Jesus Christ.*

The first step in any process is to realize what's going on so we can move forward from our old self and into God's truth and true identity for us, which is part of our transformation in Christ. I think the key to moving forward is to praise Jesus Christ no matter where we are at any point in our lives, and to know that God is completely in control of our lives, and be thankful for every part of our lives. If I think about it, I have so many reasons to be thankful. I won't dwell on the few things that are challenging in my life, but I will go to what the Word of God says for my life. I now know that Christ is working in me and through me, and building me up for His purpose. Be thankful, and have faith, and rest and dwell in His grace. God has already blessed you and me in Christ. It has already been done, so receive it. I pray His peace is a part of your life in your walk in Jesus Christ.

CHAPTER 15

His Light in You (Illuminate Your Walk)

Matthew 5:14-16 states, "You are a light of the world. A city set on a hill cannot be hidden. Nor do people light a lamp and put it under a basket, but on a stand, and it gives light to all in the house. In the same way, let your light shine before others, so that they may see your good works and give glory to your Father who is in heaven." In Christ we are now His light in this world of darkness. We should feel His peace, confidence, and courage to stand up and be who we are in Jesus Christ, utilizing the full armor of God. We are to be a light not only in our own life, but also in the lives of others who come in our path. This is a gift from God and it glorifies God when we touch others with the love of Christ. We are God's adopted children in Jesus Christ, who is the light of this world, forever. The apostle Matthew is sharing the truth about our place in this world, as believers in Jesus Christ, encouraging believers to be a light in this sometimes dark place. We should always stand up for what is true, and what is giving and loving, and be compelled to give that light to others as Christ coming through us. Christ will be manifested into our daily walks and our truth in Christ, as Christ is coming through us and out of all who believe and walk in His truth. Never hide your light and your love for others. We get the opportunity to shine the love of God, Jesus Christ, and the Holy Spirit on others. What a blessing!

It is written in Romans 8:1-2, "There is therefore now no condemnation for those who are in Christ Jesus. For the law of the Spirit of life has set you free in Christ Jesus from the law of sin and death." We talked about this in an earlier chapter, which is to know in our spirits and our hearts that we are set free in Christ. There is truly nothing that can, and will, hold us back in the grace and love of Jesus Christ, except our old self. For the law of the spirit of life has set us free in Christ Jesus from the law of sin and death. We now get to move forward into this freedom of life, once and for all, and establish our walk in Christ, in us and through us. There is no condemnation at all for those of us who are in Christ. Look to Christ if you are not in Christ, and take this opportunity to give your heart to Christ once and for all. If you have not received Christ as your Lord and Savior, you are still condemned by the law, and of sin and death.

If you are still reading, and not saved in Christ and born again, I believe that God is talking to your heart right now. *If you are ready to be a born again Christian and a child of God right now, then turn to Him and repent for your sins and ask for forgiveness through Jesus Christ, and pray to Jesus Christ to be your Lord and Savior, and ask him to come into your heart and spirit, and believe in this truth and walk in His truth for you. I pray that you will be saved and be born again in this very moment of your life.*

Psalm 27:1 states, "The Lord is my light and my salvation; whom shall I fear? The Lord is the stronghold of my life; of whom shall I be afraid?" Fear is something that most people have dealt with in their lives at one point or another, or face even on a daily basis. I know that anxieties and fears don't come from God. We don't come into this planet with fear; it is a result of living on this planet in the flesh. This psalm has always been a place in the Word of God that brings me back to the truth of peace that God and Jesus Christ has set for my life. The Lord is my light in every way, and I pray always to know and live this through grace, and to walk in the truth that has already been given to me, and for those who believe in Jesus Christ as their Lord and Savior. As believers we have been given the strength to walk in whatever challenge that has presented itself in our lives through faith, on a second by second basis. I must always remind myself of this truth that the scriptures give to all of us who believe. "Whom shall I fear?"

The Lord is my stronghold, which can mean iron grip, and the Lord won't ever let go of me. It is such a blessing to know that God, Jesus Christ and the Holy Spirit will never let go of you or me for eternity. This always brings me back to where I'm supposed to be, and that's in His peace and His rest. I'm not exactly sure how I get off track sometimes, but I know that God wants me to always stay focused on Him and Christ. I believe there is always purpose for my life, even when I get off track, as God works in all areas of my life. The truth is, that we can always get back on track in Christ, because He never let go of us in the first place. God hasn't ever, and never will leave or forsake us, and is always there for us. That is true peace. As you walk in the path of your life and your truth in Jesus Christ, always fall back on this truth and in no way leave it as it will give you strength when fear attacks. Psalm 119:105 states, "Your word is a lamp to my feet." The Word of God is light to our walk. Stay in the Word constantly in your life and it will guide your walk and your path, and you will illuminate this truth in your life.

Isaiah 49:6 states, "I will make you as a light for the nations that my salvation may reach to the end of the earth." We, as believers, are now an example of the fragrance of Jesus Christ, so people who don't know Jesus Christ can see Christ through us as 'ambassadors' of Him. This is such an incredible honor for me. We get to share Christ with others, not only in word and testimony, but in our actions, and through how we love others, and this glorifies God. This is a big part of my life and the truth in Christ as I move forward in my path in Christ. To live in the opportunity that God has given me to be caring, giving, and loving towards others, especially people who don't know me. It isn't something I do purposefully in my walk in Christ, and His fruits naturally flow from me, as Christ comes out of me. I encourage you to pray for His fruits to come out of you on a daily basis. Watch how your life will start to change and your interaction with others will be magnified in Jesus Christ.

Our lives in Christ are not about us anymore. It's about the glory of God through Christ coming through us. We are His Ambassadors on Earth for the world to see, and this is a gift for me, but it's not about me, it's about Christ in me and through me. The Holy Spirit dwells inside us, for those who have received the Holy Spirit and the Spirit will manifest Christ into our daily walks. I was such a controlling person, meaning I was always thinking about controlling every situation regarding my life, but I realized that I was never in control. When I did try and control things, I was not truly at the level of faith that I needed to be. I realize now that God is my source for everything, and when I make it about my efforts I start to turn away from that truth. Everything is for God's glory, through Christ, and through His children through

Christ. God wants His salvation in Christ to reach all corners of the earth through His children and the Word of God. It is written in 1 John 1:5-7, "this is the message we have heard from him and proclaim to you, that God is light, and in him is no darkness at all. If we say we have fellowship with him while we walk in darkness, we lie and do not practice the truth. But if we walk in the light, as he is in the light, we have fellowship with one another, and the blood of Jesus his Son cleanses us from all sin."

John 8:12 states, "Again Jesus spoke to them, saying, I am the light of the world. Whoever follows me will not walk in darkness, but will have the light of life." As you walk in your truth in Jesus Christ, remember that Jesus Christ is the light of the world and this world is full of darkness. There is no other answer or way out of the darkness of sin except through Christ. If you are in Christ, you will dwell and enjoy the light of life, which is the body of Christ for eternity, and Christ will shine out of you. Please think about this truth when life brings you down. Christ is our strength and our only hope and true source of life itself and everything in it.

Romans 13:12 states, "The night is far gone; the day is at hand. So then let us cast off the works of darkness and put on the armor of light." I like to think about armor as a shield. Can you wrap your mind around the idea of a shield of light? Nothing can penetrate the armor of Christ's light or radiance. It is so bright that no darkness can dwell inside this light. We have been given this gift through Jesus Christ, so do what the Word says and "put it on." Once you have accepted Christ's armor of light, all the works or darkness can be cast off through Christ.

Walk in love as Ephesians 5:1-2 says, "Therefore be imitators of God, as beloved children. And walk in love, as Christ loved us and gave himself up for us, a fragrant offering and sacrifice to God." To me, this is what it comes down to, and that's love. Not just the love we had before Christ was in our lives, but Jesus Christ's love fragrance coming out of us, and through us, to others in our lives, and to love ourselves the way Christ loves us. When walking in His light, we will imitate God through Christ as beloved children do. God is love, so as we walk in Christ, God's love will come out of His children.

Jesus gave himself up for us who believe through faith. Now that's ultimate love. I pray always to love others as Christ has loved me. As we walk in our truth in Christ, the most important aspect of the fragrance of Christ that will come out of us is His unconditional love towards others and ourselves. God gave us the strength through the Holy Spirit and Jesus Christ to love others in a way that we have never loved anyone before. This truth is what it all comes down to. To love the Father, Jesus, and the Holy Spirit, and then letting that love pour out towards others. What a beautiful truth! To love everyone with the type of love that Jesus brought into this world. Can you imagine what this world would be like if everyone put on the fragrance of Christ and loved others like Christ loved us, and love ourselves as Christ also loves us. What I mean about loving ourselves is we can be at peace with who we are as His children in Christ. What it comes down to is this truth; it's not about me anymore, my life is happening for the glory of God and Jesus Christ through the Holy Spirit as I live my life. *This is the ultimate truth in my walk in Christ In the Great I Am.*

CHAPTER 16

In His Image In the Great I Am (Walking in My Truth in Christ Today)

1 Corinthians 8:1 states, "Now concerning food offered to idols: we know that all of us possess knowledge. This knowledge puffs up, but love builds up." I am blessed to be an encourager and motivator of people, and a chosen Ambassador for Christ in Christ. This book's purpose is to encourage all who read it to walk in their identity and truth in Christ, but it's not just about me encouraging you, it's about the Holy Spirit stirring you up in Christ through encouraging words of truth. My truth in Christ has turned my life into a life of encouragement and love towards people that God brings into my life. My life vision in Christ, and through Christ, has manifested itself in so many purposeful ways as I am constantly being transformed in Christ by my Father in heaven through the Holy Spirit. I still fall short sometimes, but I am not a slave to sin anymore, and I now live His truth for my life. I am still confronted with anxieties and fears, but the Word of God, the

Holy Spirit, and prayer brings me out of these attacks much quicker, as my awareness of them and my understanding of my identity in Christ is what I stand on.

There are times in my life when I am still unsure of where I am going, but I always go back to two things: prayer and spending time in the Word of God. Through faith, these keep me locked into the highest purpose in my life- my relationship with my Father in heaven, Jesus Christ, and the Holy Spirit, and how I dwell in the Word of God which is alive in my life. I am in a state of devotion to Jesus Christ and His Word, and this truth drives my life forward in Christ. As I said before, I don't like leaving home without my Bible or the Word of God in the form of cards filled with scriptures, and even when I sleep, I put my Bible right next to me while God's Word lives in my heart, spirit, and mind.

I now know that my spirit is sanctified in Christ as I am being anointed through faith in Jesus Christ to write this book for God's glory. I have never written a book before, and have never had any serious training or education when it comes to writing books. Most of this book is my shared testimony and my commentary regarding God's Word, with a foundation and vision of walking in my truth in Christ. God is sovereign and knows exactly where I am, and I have faith that He works in my life all the time. I believe the more I dwell in His Word and pray to Him, the more I will discern and have an understanding of His purpose for me in His Kingdom for His glory.

If you notice, this book is focused on scripture and my thoughts about God's gospel of Jesus Christ. I am not a pastor or a minister, but I am an Ambassador of Jesus Christ, and I have been appointed by God, as an heir in Christ, and I am a saint in Christ, and so are all of you who are in Christ. This is number one for me in my life; that I am in Christ.

His fragrance and fruit comes out of me, not because of anything I do, but from what Christ does through me. John 15:5 states, "I am the Vine: you are the branches. Whoever believes in me and I in him bears much fruit. However, apart from me you can do nothing." This is an important truth, that we can't do anything without God. The Lord Jesus Christ is our ultimate source for everything in life. God loves us so very much, in fact our understanding of the measure of love that God has for us comes from His Son Jesus Christ and how He died on the cross for my sins and your sins.

So as I start to share where I am in my truth in the 'Great I Am,' I hope that as you've read this book, it shows you where my heart is, and hopefully you can assess where your heart is as well. My faith is in, and comes from, Jesus Christ. This book is all about my faith in Christ, through the Word of God. This book is a manifestation of Christ in me, for God's glory, and Christ's glory, and is now a part of my life in Christ in every way. Writing this book has been an incredible gift for me and I believe this is just the next stage of my journey In the Great I Am. I have become a national public speaker and an inspirational and business coach, and my prayer is that God will continue to put me into the world in His light and for His glory. I truly believe my purpose is to speak about Jesus Christ and be a Barnabas or an encourager for all the people that God puts in front of me, and encourage everyone who has ears to hear about the incredible truth and gift of reconciliation through belief and faith in Jesus Christ through grace.

My purpose is to dwell in His truth at all times, and be used by God to touch other lives with the love of the gospel through encouragement. Through the Father, Jesus Christ, and the Holy Spirit, I am now able to live and walk in these truths, and love and support my brothers and sisters in Christ, and encourage and ignite them in all areas of their lives for God's glory. Through the Holy Spirit and faith in Jesus Christ, God is building a foundation for me based on scripture. This truth is the basis of encouragement and knowledge through love, which is where God has me at this point in my life. The biggest truth in my life is the truth of the gospel and the gift of Jesus Christ and His grace and walking daily in His truth, as I move forward in my truth, *In the Great I Am*. I am in prayer that God will continue to utilize the heart I have to elevate people in their truth in Christ. Utilizing my speaking abilities and the gift of encouragement, I want to continue to reach out to all people that Christ brings to me for His Glory. Please pray for me.

My truth and purpose in Christ has always been my love for my family which God has blessed me with. I pray that every day I am dwelling in His truth and His perfect love, and that it comes out of me when I am being a husband to my wife Rori, and a father to my daughter Mariah and my son Luke. One of the most important truths for me *In the Great I Am,* is walking Christ like with my family, with the love of Jesus in me at all times. For those of you who are blessed to have children and a spouse, I want to remind you of the true gift of family. It is truly a blessing from God that you are a part of something as special as family. As a father, I know that God guides me through every step of the process of raising my children, and understanding their needs along with loving them in a Christ like way, so that they know they are loved and protected and they can truly walk in the truth of their lives.

One of the biggest gifts that I have been given by God is to know that both of my children have accepted Jesus Christ in their hearts and are saved forever. It brings me so much peace to know this truth, and I thank God for His grace on my children. In fact, my wife and I both accepted Jesus Christ into our hearts at the same exact moment in time and place. How cool is that to know that God called us into His family together, in that very same moment? Our marriage covenant in Christ has been a blessing, although it can be challenging at times, as any relationship can be, but God always brings us back to a place of love and peace in our relationship and marriage, which starts with focusing on Christ first. My wife Rori and I are not only married, but we are best friends, and we are brothers and sisters in Christ. Being blessed to be able to love and share my life with my family is a huge part of my truth in Christ.

As I look at my path in Christ, and how God is working in my life in Christ, I have been so blessed over the last twelve years to have been able to play worship music for God and Jesus Christ with my church. I truly believe that this is one of my purposes in Christ, because worship is about glorifying God and letting go. I love to worship and play music on the drums for the Lord because it takes me out of myself and into worship, which is where I always want to be. I'm not thinking about anything else except Jesus Christ and worshiping Him and our Father in heaven. The Holy Spirit guides me in worship. Sometimes I'm not sure of what's happening in the music, but the Holy Spirit gives me discernment about the worship and the music in Christ, and the rhythm of what is being said. It seems like I've been playing it all my life. It's truly a gift from God to be able to be on a worship team, and to be able to serve in this type of ministry for the Lord. I cherish it. I thank you so much Jesus.

Walking in my truth in Christ for me is to walk in my purpose and destiny in Christ for His glory. This has always been my purpose from when God decided to create and form me, before time even existed, and this is true for all of us who believe. It's absolutely incredible and such a glorious blessing to walk in God's purpose, and a truth which is actually the will of God. The truth is, if you are reading these words, it has been ordained by God for you to do so. Believe. When we are born, we lose our way as we are born into a sin nature on this planet, but through Christ and being born again, we find our way back into our truth and purpose in Christ for His glory. It's a beautiful truth.

18 years ago God gave me a big responsibility and a gift of working with young people. I have always loved sports all my life, especially basketball. I was brought into coaching by a great Christian friend as a freshman boy's basketball coach. I was mentored for two years, and then was invited to coach under the varsity boys basketball coach who was another Christian brother for four years. At that point, the Lord really shook things up in my life and brought an opportunity to be the head varsity girls basketball coach at a local high school. I could see the Lord working in this because of the events that transpired and the amount of outpouring from the local community for me to a part of these kids' lives. I finished seven years as the Head Varsity Girls Coach, and it was truly a blessing from God that I got to be a part of these kids' lives for all this time. Over the last 5 years, I have returned back to coaching the boys with my original coaching mentor, and it has been a gift to work with young people and show them the fragrance of Jesus Christ through me every single day. I am so thankful that the Lord brought this gift into my life, and I truly believe that this is one of the truths in my life vision *In the Great I Am*.

Jesus Christ is flowing out of my life in every way and I'm being transformed to trust and not control. I'm thankful for Jesus Christ for everything in my life, especially His love and patience for me. My job has been a blessing in so many ways, but especially because I've gotten to bring who I truly am into every situation at work through Christ and the Holy Spirit. I am now a National Business Coach for my company, as God continues to bless me to be an encourager and support others. I pray that people see Christ in me and through me. This is what dwelling in the truth in Christ is all about to me. Christ coming out of me in everything I do, in every relationship, every conversation, every celebration, every victory, every tribulation, every defeat, every thought, and every breath. Christ in me and through me *In the Great I Am*. Praise Jesus.

Joshua 22:5 states, "Only be very careful to observe the commandment and the law that Moses the servant of the Lord commanded you, to love the Lord your God, and to walk in all his ways to keep his commandments and to cling to him and to serve him with all your heart and with all your soul." In our truth in Christ, let's make sure to remember and pray so that we always cling to Him, and to serve Him with all our heart and with all our soul. It's not about us anymore, it's about the Father, Jesus Christ our Lord and the Holy Spirit as we are in Christ, and Christ is in God. *This is our transformation from our old self to our new self in Christ In the Great I Am.* God Bless you all.

CHAPTER 17

Amazing Grace
(Christ the Grace giver is the
Reason for Our Life in Christ)

Romans 12:3-8 states, "For by the grace given to me I say to every-one among you not to think of himself more highly than he ought to think, but to think with sober judgment, each according to the mea-sure of faith that God has assigned. For as in one body we have many members, and the members do not all have the same function, so we, though many, are one body in Christ, and individually members one of another. Having gifts that differ according to the grace given to us, let us use them: if prophecy, in proportion to our faith; if service, in our serving; the one who teaches, in his teaching; the one who exhorts, in his exhortation; the one who contributes, in generosity; the one who leads, with zeal; the one who does acts of mercy, with cheerfulness."

The main thing that really stands out to me in this scripture is to make sure, as we move forward in our truth in Christ, that we stay humble in every way to those who believe, and for the people who haven't believed yet. We must never put ourselves above anyone or in front of anyone else, and above all be sober minded about any potential judgment towards others. Be very conscious about how we feel about others and remember that God gave us His grace through Jesus Christ, through nothing that you or I have done on our own. There are many members of the body of Christ. Christ is the head and the members don't have the same function, purpose, or role, but we are one body in Christ for God's glory not our own. God has blessed us all with different gifts for His purpose, but He says that we need to use them. This is an important scripture that I would like to discuss. It is basically saying that if you have been given a gift, you are to 'use it.' Don't wait to use your gifts. 1 Peter 4:10 states, "As each has received a gift, use it to serve one another, as good stewards of God's varied grace: whoever speaks, as one who speaks oracles of God; whoever serves by the strength that God supplies – in order that in everything God may be glorified through Jesus Christ."

When walking in our truth in Christ and through Christ, I believe our gifts will shine out of all of us who believe, towards everyone else around us as the fragrance of Christ comes out of us. This is an important step in the process of walking in our truth in Christ, as we were already appointed in Christ before the beginning of time. Our gifts were already established before we even had life, so those gifts that come out of us in Christ are for a specific Godly intention which is God's purpose for His glory for His Kingdom. I encourage all of you to walk in your gifts through prayer and the encouragement of the Holy Spirit through the grace of Jesus Christ. Ephesians 2:8 states, "For by grace you have been saved through faith. And this is not your own doing; it is the gift of God, not a result of works, so that no one may boast. For we are his workmanship, created in Christ Jesus for good works, which God prepared beforehand, that we should walk in them."

It is written in Titus 2:11-14, "For the grace of God has appeared, bringing salvation for all people, training us to renounce ungodliness and worldly passions, and to live self-controlled, upright, and godly lives in the present age, waiting for our blessed hope, the appearing of the glory of our great God and Savior Jesus Christ, who gave himself for us to redeem us from all lawlessness and to purify for himself a people for his own possession who are zealous for good works." What excites me about this passage of scripture is that the grace of God has appeared through Jesus Christ, bringing salvation for all who believe, through the grace of Jesus Christ. I pray that all people will experience this grace and salvation in their lives. Grace is from God, and it is an undeserved and unmerited favor towards us who believe through Jesus Christ. I love this with all I have, as it gives me hope that every person can be saved through the grace of Jesus Christ. Through grace we can live a holy life right now, and not just wait for heaven, as Jesus Christ is coming through us.

God wants us to be zealous, passionate, and enthusiastic about choosing the right path in our lives. I now realize that doing the right thing is actually Christ in me, leading my life through the Holy Spirit to be Christ like. Let's all grow in our truth in Jesus Christ in every way. We can do it, as Christ in us can do anything. Choices matter in life as God gives us free moral authority to choose. I truly believe I am being led to share these words with all of you for His glory. Galatians 4:19 states, "My little children, for whom I am again in the anguish of childbirth until Christ is formed in you!" *The Holy Spirit is guiding and showing me how to live my life in Christ, as Christ is being formed in me every minute of my life.*

Hebrews 2:9 states, "But we see him who for a little while he was made lower than the angels, namely Jesus, crowned with glory and honor because of the suffering of death, so that by the grace of God he might taste death for everyone." Jesus is crowned with all glory and honor from the Father, as Jesus tasted death once and for all for us who believe in Him. Through grace we won't feel the sting of death in Christ if we are truly in Him. Jesus took all of our sins, and is now our propitiation for all of us who believe through faith. God brought grace to humanity through Jesus Christ so that we, who believe, could be righteous in Christ for eternity through faith. God's grace had to start with the suffering of death of His own Son Jesus Christ on the cross. I am actually fighting back tears right now thinking about my own son, and what that would mean to me and how big a sacrifice that would be. This sacrifice is at the heart of God's grace and mercy for us. God gave up His only Son Jesus Christ to be crucified on a cross for those who would believe in His name as their Lord and Savior. This is amazing grace.

Galatians 2:21 says, "I do not nullify the grace of God, for if righteousness were through the law, then Christ died for no purpose." I am in Christ because of His loving unmerited grace, through this unconditional sacrifice of God's Son Jesus Christ. Grace was bought at the highest price, and we should thank God for this grace that was freely given to us. Grace comes from a God that is full of grace, and I in no way deserved this grace. This truth impacts my heart in every way. Ephesians 4:7 states, "But grace was given to each one of us according to the measure of Christ's gift."

Titus 3:7 states, "So that being justified by his grace we might become heirs according to the hope of eternal life." We have already discussed the truth about the believer's justification in Christ through grace, and the reality of its blessings, but to become an heir in Christ of the Father in heaven is breathtaking. If we are heirs of God in Jesus Christ, then we are able to receive all the gifts, authority, blessings and we now have the identity as children of God through Jesus Christ. Every blessing in Christ has now been established to all of us who believe in Jesus Christ, as long as we are truly in Christ. We are God's heirs or His benefactors in Christ Jesus. Think about that for a while and let your heart settle in that truth, and be in peace and allow yourself to rest in it. If you believe in Jesus Christ as your Lord and Savior you are adopted in Christ. Psalm 45:2 states, "You are the most handsome of the sons of men; grace is poured upon your lips; therefore God has blessed you forever." Grace has been poured on our lips through Christ, and we have therefore been blessed forever by God because of His grace through Jesus Christ.

2 Timothy 2:1 states, "You then, my child, be strengthened by the grace that is in Christ Jesus and what you have heard from me in the presence of many witnesses entrust to faithful men who will be able to teach others also." When we walk in our truth in Christ we are strengthened and edified by the grace that is in Christ Jesus. We have taken on the grace of Jesus Christ in our lives right now as we are in Christ. Christ's grace in us through Jesus Christ *In the Great I Am.*

Romans 6:14 states, "For sin will have no dominion over you, since you are not under law but under grace." Sin will no longer rule our lives through Christ, as grace has been given to the believer. John 1:17 states, "For the law was given through Moses; grace and truth came through Jesus Christ." Through Jesus Christ grace will bring our lives to a place of fruit and peace because of the grace that is in Christ, and is now in us through faith. We don't have to do anything except believe in Christ, dwell in His Word, and constantly pray, and His grace will shine out of us. Sin no longer has any power over our lives, as we are no longer slaves to sin in Christ. We are not under the law, but under grace, which is like having a grace blanket on all of us who believe. All of us in Jesus Christ are all blanketed with grace in our lives, so live in this truth and focus on the grace in you.

2 Corinthians 12:9 says, "But he said to me, my grace is sufficient for you, for my power is made perfect in weakness." We will all fall short on a daily basis, but we don't have to worry about it, as Christ's power is made perfect in our weakness. Even when we fall short, the grace of Jesus Christ fills the void or gap of our weakness, and we are perfect in God's eyes. Wow, what a beautiful gift and truth. I hope you all hold onto this beautiful truth for the rest of eternity in Christ. Hebrews 4:16 states, "Let us then with confidence draw near to the throne of grace, that we may receive mercy and find grace to help in time of need."

2 Peter 3:18 states, "But grow in the grace and knowledge of our Lord and Savior Jesus Christ. To him be the glory both now and to the day of eternity. Amen." Let us always give thanks, and know we are under His grace, as we walk in our truth in Christ for Christ. I pray I continue to grow in His grace that is now in me, and the knowledge of His truth for my life in Christ. Let's always give God the glory, both now and till the day of eternity. Praise you Jesus, and praise you Father, and the Holy Spirit. Thank you for my life in Christ, for Christ through Grace. Ephesians 1:6 states, "To the praise of his glorious grace, with which he has blessed us in the Beloved." 2 Thessalonians 3:18 states, "The grace of our Lord Jesus Christ be with you all." I pray that the grace of our Lord and Savior Jesus Christ will be with all of you for eternity. In Christ you are saved through this most beautiful truth and gift to mankind. I believe the greatest gift for mankind in all of history is grace given to us through Jesus Christ from our Father in Heaven. *Christ is Grace. Believe and receive!*

CHAPTER 18

Why it Matters So Much (A Bridge of Hope for Unbelievers and Believers)

It is written in Philippians 3:12-21, "Not that I have already obtained this or am already perfect, but I press on to make it my own, because Christ Jesus has made me his own. Brothers, I do not consider that I have made it my own. But one thing I do: forgetting what lies behind and straining forward to what lies ahead, I press on toward the goal for the prize of the upward call of God in Christ Jesus. Let those of us who are mature think this way, and if in anything you think otherwise, God will reveal that also to you. Only let us hold true to what we have attained. Brothers, join in imitating me, and keep your eyes on those who walk according to the example you have in us. For many, of whom I have often told you and now tell you even with tears, walk as enemies of the cross of Christ. Their end is destruction, their god is their belly, and they glory in their shame, with minds set on earthly things. But our citizenship is in heaven, and from it we await a Savior, the Lord Jesus

Christ, who will transform our lowly body to be like his glorious body, by the power that enables him even to subject all things to himself."

I am living my life in Christ, and Christ is in me and coming out of me, and I am being transformed to be like Christ every day of my life through my walk in Jesus Christ and the Holy Spirit. Jesus Christ is absolutely perfect in every way, and He is in those who believe, including me. We who believe are in Christ, and Christ is in God, and God is in Christ. We who believe in Jesus Christ as our Lord and Savior are all connected to Christ; if connected and in Christ, then we are also in God through Christ, and He has made us His very own for all eternity. Remember this moving forward on your journey. Walk in the truth of your life in Christ, and finish your race put in front you. Dwell with Christ for eternity and your upward call of Christ for your life. Those who are in Christ have citizenship and residency in heaven with our Lord and Savior Jesus Christ. The same power that He subjects to Himself will change our lowly, earthly bodies to be like His glorious body forever.

1 Peter 1:3-9 states, "Blessed be the God and Father of our Lord Jesus Christ! According to his great mercy, he has caused us to be born again to a living hope through the resurrection of Jesus Christ from the dead, to an inheritance that is imperishable, undefiled, and unfading, kept in heaven for you, who by God's power are being guarded through faith for a salvation ready to be revealed in the last time. In this you rejoice, though now for a little while, if necessary, you have been grieved by various trials, so that the tested genuineness of your faith---more precious than gold that perishes though it is tested by fire--- may be found to result in praise and glory and honor at the revelation of Jesus Christ. Though you have not seen him, you love him. Though you do not now see him, you believe in him and rejoice with joy that

is inexpressible and filled with glory, obtaining the outcome for your faith, the salvation of your souls."

Walking in our truth in Jesus Christ is about knowing this reality once and for all, and to dwell through belief and faith in the grace of our Lord and Savior Jesus Christ. God has caused us to be born again to a living hope through His Son Jesus Christ, to an inheritance that is undefiled and unfading, which means it will never go away, kept in heaven, for those who believe through faith. We will be tested and we will face challenges and trials in our life, but stay true to your genuine faith and belief which is more precious than anything in this world. We love Jesus and are joyful in every way as we walk in our truth in Christ.

In Jesus Christ we are saved.

Called to Be Holy

1 Peter 1:13-23 states, "Therefore, preparing your minds for action, and being sober-minded, set your hope fully on the grace that will be brought to you at the revelation of Jesus Christ. As obedient children, do not be conformed to the passions of your former ignorance, but as he who called you is holy, you also be holy in all your conduct, since it is written, "You shall be holy, for I am holy." And if you call on him as Father who judges impartially according to each one's deeds, conduct yourselves with fear throughout the time of your exile, knowing that you were ransomed from the futile ways inherited from your forefathers, not with perishable things such as silver or gold, but with the precious blood of Christ, like that of a lamb without blemish or spot. He was foreknown before the foundation of the world but was made manifest in the last times for the sake of you who through him are believers in God, who raised him from the dead and gave him glory,

so that your faith and hope are in God. Having purified your souls by your obedience to the truth for a sincere brotherly love, love one another earnestly from a pure heart, since you have been born again, not of perishable seed but of imperishable, through the living and abiding word of God." God is calling us to be Holy in Christ by walking in our truth in Christ. God wants us to prepare and renew our minds, as we talked about in a previous chapter. God wants us to keep a clear mind, with our hope fully on the grace of Jesus Christ through Jesus Christ. We should never go back to the way we used to be, before we were saved in Christ, but to be Holy in our conduct in Christ, through the power of the Holy Spirit and grace. We should always remember that we who believe were ransomed or bought by the precious blood of Jesus Christ. *We weren't paid for by anything of this world, but by the precious blood of the Son of God.* Our faith and hope are in God having believed in the truth of the grace of Jesus Christ as our Lord and Savior, with the Holy Spirit dwelling in us sealed in the truth of Jesus Christ. As we walk in Christ, our Father is guiding us and showing us how to live a holy life through the Holy Spirit, and the truth of the Word of God, which is living and abiding forever in us right now. We have the genuine love and grace of Jesus Christ in us first, and most importantly, and we can now, in Christ, share Christ's love with all others. Christ's love is a pure love that is untainted and comes from an unstained heart, since we now love through Jesus Christ. The Word of the Lord lives forever. This book is living because it is full of the Word of God. Thank you Father God, Jesus Christ my Lord, and the Holy Spirit. Praise you.

The Mission Field

Matthew 4:19 states, "follow me, and I will make you fishers of men." One of the gifts of this book for me was to be able to prepare myself to become a fisher of men in my truth in Christ to the masses. I pray to the Lord that if one person or millions of people could hear these words, and be touched by the Holy Spirit to believe in Christ, I would be so thankful to be used by God for His glory and for the glory of Jesus Christ. The journey and the time I spent in prayer, and in the Spirit writing this book, was a gift from God for me. My journey writing this book supported a higher level of intimacy for me with the Holy Spirit, Jesus Christ, and my Father in heaven. I now know I am being transformed to have a deeper understanding as to what my identity in Christ for His glory truly is. I now understand that everyone's truth in Christ is to become a fisherman of men and women, for the Kingdom of Jesus Christ, and to share the gift of grace and reconciliation as an Ambassador for Jesus Christ with love for everyone as Christ loves us and flows through us.

When walking in Christ we will become fishers of men naturally as Christ's nature will be flowing out of us. Matthew 28:18-20 were the last words that Matthew records for us that Jesus spoke, "all authority in heaven and on earth has been given to me. Go therefore and make disciples of all nations, baptizing them in the name of the Father and of the Son and of the Holy Spirit, teaching them to observe all that I have commanded you. And behold, I am with you always, to the end of the age."

1 Timothy 2:3-6 states, "this is good, and it is pleasing in the sight of God our Savior, who desires all people to be saved and to come to the knowledge of the truth. For there is one God, and there is one mediator between God and men, the man Christ Jesus, who gave himself as a ransom for all, which is the testimony given at the proper time." This is one of the scriptures that truly touches me in such a powerful way of encouragement. Paul is sharing with us that it's our Savior's desire

for "all" people to be saved, and to come to the knowledge of the truth concerning His grace. Christ is the mediator between God and man. *Jesus Christ is our bridge to God through grace.* This is one of my truths in Christ. I believe it will become yours as well, unless it already is, and that it is to share the good news about Jesus Christ and the gospel with others, especially people close to you, so they may know the truth, and believe, and be saved in Christ. This scripture has changed my life, and I believe it is one of the main reasons I was led to write this book and commentary through the Holy Spirit about my truth in Christ.

God's Glory

1 Corinthians 10:31 states, "So whatever you eat or drink, or whatever you do, do all to the glory of God." 1 Corinthians 11:1 tells us, "Be imitators of me, as I am of Christ." Paul is telling us to be an imitator of him, as he is not seeking anything for his own good, but to perform the will of God for the glory of God. Paul is of Christ. In everything we do it should be to the 100% glory of God, and not ourselves. This is a strong compass for the believer, and that is to ask ourselves this simple question- is what I'm doing right now glorifying God? The only way this can be approached is to know that our strength is from Christ, through the Holy Spirit, so the nature of Christ comes out of us which gives glory to God. Think of the needs of many and not just ourselves, for those who believe in Christ. Psalm 72:19 reads, "blessed be his glorious name forever; may the whole earth be filled with his glory! Amen and Amen."

Psalm 96:3-4 states, "declare his glory among the nations, his marvelous works among all the peoples! For great is the Lord, and greatly to be praised." Our Lord is deserving of all the glory among the nations, and all the people, and we should live our lives praising Him at all times through Jesus Christ. Give all the glory for your lives in Christ to our Lord and Savior Jesus Christ, and the grace of God. Living in our truth *In the Great I Am* is about giving and living our lives to glorify our Lord and Savior Jesus Christ, and praising and thanking Him for the gift of everlasting life that He has given to those who believe in His Word through faith.

His Purpose For Me

2 Peter 1:3-12 tells us, "His divine power has granted to us all things that pertain to life and godliness, through the knowledge of him who called us to his own glory and excellence, by which he has granted to us his precious and very great promises, so that through them you may become partakers of the divine nature, having escaped from the corruption that is in the world because of sinful desire. For this very reason, make every effort to supplement your faith with virtue, and virtue with knowledge, and knowledge with self-control, and self-control with steadfastness, and steadfastness with godliness, and godliness with brotherly affection, and brotherly affection with love. For if these qualities are yours and are increasing, they keep you from being ineffective or unfruitful in the knowledge of our Lord Jesus Christ. For whoever lacks these qualities is so nearsighted that he is blind, having forgotten that he was cleansed from his former sins. Therefore, brothers, be all the more diligent to make your calling and election sure, for if you practice these qualities you will never fall. For in this way there will be richly provided for you an entrance into the eternal kingdom of our Lord and Savior Jesus Christ. Therefore I intend always to remind you of these qualities, though you know them and are established in the truth that you have."

This scripture tells me everything about who I am in Christ, and the truth of His blessing for how I want to live my life and for those who believe. Just read it again and again until you truly feel the Holy Spirit stir your soul and spirit before moving on. Peter tells us that we have been granted, or what I would say is approved or established, and given all things that pertain to life and godliness, through the knowledge of Him who called us into His own glory and magnificence and splendor. Let's just stop there for a minute and really take a look at this blessing and this awesome truth of His willingness to share His total nature with us; His children in Christ. This truth needs to be truly accepted in our hearts and minds in Christ, for us to truly start to live in the nature of Christ, and in His purpose for us doing kingdom business for God's glory. Romans 14:17 states, "For the kingdom of God is not a matter of eating and drinking but of righteousness and peace and joy in the Holy Spirit." Jesus told us in Matthew 6:33, "But seek first the kingdom of God and his righteousness, and all these things will be added to you." Walking in Christ gives us everything we need to put the kingdom of God and His righteousness first in everything we do. We've now escaped and died from the corruption of this world through Jesus Christ in our new walk of truth and salvation in Jesus Christ. *Let us walk in peace, joy, and righteousness in Christ for God's glory.*

When walking *In the Great I Am*, I pray for you to have guidance and strength of the Holy Spirit, and a true focus on the Word of God through the Holy Spirit and Jesus Christ. Jesus wants us all to be beneficial in the knowledge of Him so we can glorify God in everything we do, for and in the kingdom of Christ. Jesus tells us in Matthew 25:31-41, "When the Son of Man comes in his glory, and all the angels with him, then he will sit on his glorious throne. Before him will be gathered all the nations, and he will separate people one from another as a shepherd separates the sheep from the goats. And he will place the sheep on his right, but the goats on the left. Then the King will say to those on his right, 'come, you who are blessed by my Father, inherit the kingdom prepared for you from the foundation of the world. For I was hungry and you gave me food, I was thirsty and you gave me drink, I was a stranger and you welcomed me, I was naked and you clothed me, I was sick and you visited me, I was in prison and you came to me.' Then the righteous will answer him, saying, 'Lord, when did we see you hungry and feed you, or thirsty and give you drink? And when did we see you a stranger and welcome you, or naked and clothe you? And when did we see you sick or in prison and visit you? And the King will answer them, 'Truly, I say to you, as you did it to one of the least of these my brothers, you did it to me."

Can you picture what it's going to be like when Christ comes in all His glory and wonder and beauty in the Second Advent? It will be glorious in every way. Every single nation will be gathered in front of Him and all His angels, and He will separate all the people once and for all. God's Kingdom has been established since the beginning of the world, before time even existed. Christ is telling us clearly how to walk in Him. *Jesus is showing us to love and take care of those who can't take care of themselves.*

Walking *In the Great I Am* and my truth in Christ is a manifestation of my life in Christ through Christ. To glorify God in everything I do and say, and about me being self-less, and thinking of and loving others more than I love myself, just like Jesus Christ did. Jesus gave Himself up on a cross for those who would believe. I now live my life for the glory of God, and our Lord and Savior Jesus Christ, with the power of the Holy Spirit guiding me, encouraging me, and strengthening me. To not only walk in Christ, but to realize that we are now 'one' with the Holy Spirit and our Lord and Savior Jesus Christ, and now one with God. The nature of Jesus Christ is constantly coming out of us who are in Him. Jesus Christ is the image of God, and we are now the image of Jesus Christ. So go and walk *In the Great I Am* and He will flow out of you for eternity, as your truth in Christ is Christ through you. *Jesus is the way, and the truth, and the life. Praise Jesus Christ every moment of your life. Christ in you and through you is what it means to walk In the Great I Am.*

Revelations 1:8 reveals, "I am the Alpha and the Omega, says the Lord God, who is and who was and who is to come, the Almighty." We who believe in Jesus Christ are now in the Alpha and the Omega, who is, and who was, and who is to come, the Almighty. *We are dwelling and living In the Great I Am through Jesus Christ for eternity for God's glory.* I pray that you all just soak this beautiful truth in, once and for all. In Christ you are now able to live a life full of love, peace, and blessings. In Christ you have been given His authority over your life, and you can now move that forward, and be a blessing for others through the nature and truth of Jesus Christ in you.

Our Lord and Savior Jesus Christ is love, and is the reason for life itself. In Jesus Christ you are now love. Don't hold back, and share His love with others. This is now your identity in Jesus Christ.

I pray blessings and love to all of you through Jesus Christ, and I pray that you are living in your truth and walking *In the Great I Am.* God bless you my brothers and sisters, and I pray that you will always love all people, and rest in the peace of Jesus Christ in your lives as Christ lives through the new creation that is you. Be blessed all of you in Jesus Christ, and may love permeate every moment of your lives *In the Great I Am.* I pray you all have victory through Jesus Christ, as we dwell together *In the Great I Am.*

My Identity in Jesus Christ:

- I am no longer a slave to sin.

- I am saved and born again in Christ Jesus and I have the righteousness of God through Jesus Christ.

- I am an Ambassador for Christ, sharing the gift of reconciliation with others.

- I am a light in Christ for the world to see.

- Christ comes through me.

- I am a man who God is making His appeal through for others.

- I am created by God; His workmanship.

- I am loved by God. I have God's love in me.

- I am reconciled to God through faith in Jesus Christ.

- I am a father who looks to the Word of God to show me how to be a good father.

- I am a husband who has submitted to my beautiful wife and I love her like Christ loved the church.

- I am a son who has learned to understand just how much my parents really did try to give me a life that had love and opportunity.

- I am the adopted son of the Holy Father in Heaven through faith that was gracefully given to me through Jesus Christ, my Lord and Savior.

- I am a man who dwells in the Word of God and sometimes sleeps holding on to my Bible at night.

- I am a man blessed in life and business to be able to encourage and love all people I meet.

- I am in exile on this planet.

- I am a man that has been delivered through Jesus Christ from all types of strongholds in my life including the daily torture of fear and anxiety. I am now being perfected in God's love.

- I am a man who wants to serve the Lord and touch people's lives through the Gospel of Jesus Christ.

- I am a National Corporate Speaker who loves to impact people towards their purpose and destiny in Jesus Christ.

- I am a man who receives his blessings of recovery from debt once and for all.

- I am a man who has been given the gift of encouragement through the grace of God.

- I am a man of God through belief and faith in Jesus Christ.

- I am baptized in the Holy Spirit through Jesus Christ.

- I am sealed for eternity and constantly encouraged by the Holy Spirit.

- I am a man who still gets attacked by my old self and the enemy, but I know it's not from God and it's a lie.

- I am a man who knows that God has transformed and changed my life through Christ for eternity. I am a new creation, and I am being transformed from old self into a new creature in Christ through Christ.

- I am a man who has been given the anointing to encourage all of you to walk *In the Great I Am.*

- I have been given the gift of speaking in the Spirit.

- I am a man who hasn't seen much of the world yet, but I know that is coming for God's glory.

- I am a man who is clinging to God's truth as my only truth.

- I am a man who loves God with all my heart as He shows me how to love like Him.

- I am a brother to all of you in Christ through Christ.

- I am anointed by the Holy Spirit to share the Word of God with others.

- I have the resurrection power of the Holy Spirit in me, through Christ, and all things are possible and have already been manifested in Christ. The same resurrection power that raised Christ from the dead is in me.

- I receive every blessing in Christ through the faith that God has given to me.

- I am a man who has been justified with God in Christ Jesus for all time.

- I am a man who clings to every loving moment of life in Christ Jesus, and looks forward to eternity with Christ in heaven.

- I am a man on my journey to touch the masses for Christ.

- I am an Inspirational Coach for Christ and God's glory.

- I am a Business Christian Life Coach in Christ.

- I am a National Business Coach for my company to support others in walking in their potential.

- I am part of The Holy Priesthood in Jesus Christ.

- I am part of the Holy Nation in Christ Jesus.

- I was ransomed to be a part of the body of Christ. Thank you Jesus.

- I am a man who has been blessed by God to have two children, an incredible wife, and a mother and father who are saved in Christ.

- I am an heir in Christ and I am part of the Kingdom of God in Christ right now.

- I have eternal life in Christ through grace.

- I have eternal unending love from God in Christ through grace.

- I am saved from the sting of death...In Christ I will never see or feel the sting of death.

- In His Grace I have immeasurable riches in Christ.

- I am a man in Christ who has been given complete authority in Christ.

- I am a man in the Great I Am through Christ.

My Truth in Christ

God has already manifested and apportioned His fruits and gifts to all of us who believe, depending on His purpose for us for His glory. It has already been established. I don't have to go looking for it, as it is already in me, a part of me, and has always been so. I rest in His truth and pray for strength to be who I was always made to be, before the foundations of time, when I was chosen and predestined. This is fundamental and key to what the Holy Spirit has been moving through me in this commentary, and throughout this book. I now know that I am a new creature in Christ, and have already been established in my identity and all of my blessings, purposes, and truths in Christ. I have been given the Holy Spirit's resurrection power and complete authority through Jesus Christ to establish and dwell in His truth as a disciple of Jesus Christ rooted in His grace.

Jesus Christ in me is my truth in Christ, as I walk in my identity in Christ, as Christ comes through me *In the Great I Am*. His Spirit and the gifts I have, flow out of me for God's glory manifesting His light into this world. I will continue to go and walk in my truth in Christ every day. *Christ in me and through me.*

God Bless all of you and I will see you soon on the road for God's purpose and glory *In the Great I Am.*

Anthony A. Casillas
In Christ and through Christ In the Great I Am

A Letter of Gratitude

I want to take this time to thank and praise my Father God in heaven, who gave me life, and predestined me before the foundations of the world ever began to be in Christ. I want to thank you, Father God, for your grace that you gave me as a free gift. I believe and have faith in your Son Jesus Christ, and what it manifested in me as a believer through faith in Jesus Christ, who is my Lord and Savior. Praise you Jesus Christ for being my propitiation and taking on all of my sins in the past, present, and future through grace, and shedding your blood on the cross. What a blessing in my life! You are my Lord and Savior, and I am so thankful for your love and grace on and in my life. Jesus you are coming out of me through the Holy Spirit, who is always encouraging me and guiding me through the incredible truth of your Word every single moment of my life. I thank you Father God, Jesus Christ, and the Holy Spirit for the Word of God, as it is the foundation of how I live my life. The Word is now the truth for my life as a new creature in Jesus Christ. Thank you so much Holy Spirit. I praise you. You are constantly working in me, in everything I do in my life every single moment. I thank you so much for your guidance and encouragement, and being the sealer of my entrance into heaven someday. I'm so thankful to the Holy Trinity, and the ultimate truth of the Word of God which is alive and in me. You are all the foundation of my life. I love you and praise you Father God, Jesus Christ, and the Holy Spirit.

I want to thank my family, especially my mom Judy, for always loving me and being there for me in every instance of my life. Your love is a gift from God. I want to thank my dad for initially sharing and teaching me the foundational truths of the Word of God in our Bible studies together. To my beautiful wife Rori, and to my two children, Mariah and Luke, I want to let you know that you are my heartbeat and my inspiration here on this planet, besides my relationship with God, Jesus Christ, and the Holy Spirit. You have always loved me with a special love that only comes from God. Thank you for always supporting all of my dreams in my life. I love you with the love of Christ in me.

I want to thank all of the pastors that have shared their knowledge of the truth of the Word of God with me, as you are Spirit filled and anointed by God and Jesus Christ. Thank you for always supporting me in my walk in truth in Jesus Christ. I want to send a special thank you to Crenshaw Christian Center in Los Angeles California, for being the place where my wife and I accepted Jesus Christ into our lives at the exact same moment and place in time. Thank you for your love and the gift of how you shepherd and teach the Word of God to God's people and to me. I want to thank my fellow Christian brother Wogbe, for sharing the truth about grace and the gift of reconciliation with me, plus being baptized in the Holy Spirit with me in the same moment. You are truly a man of God and my brother for eternity. I would like to send a special thank you to Lele Ste for all her support and encouragement as an author and a sister in Christ. I want to thank all of my friends and brothers and sisters in Christ for your continued love and support in my walk in truth in Jesus Christ. I pray for all of you, and your families right now.

In closing, I thank all of you who have taken your precious time to read and receive these words of my testimony and commentary, which I believe I have received from the Holy Spirit and the Word of God, through my faith in Jesus Christ. I pray that the Holy Spirit has stirred up your spirit in Jesus Christ and has created and solidified a new foundation of truth in your walk *In the Great I Am*. I pray blessings on all of you and your families in the name of our Lord and Savior Jesus Christ.

God Bless all of you *In the Great I AM*,
Anthony A. Casillas
In Christ for God's Glory

#85 ~

Erik : Kathy ~

I pray you are
blessed in the great
I AM.

Be Blessed

Anthony N Wallace

#85